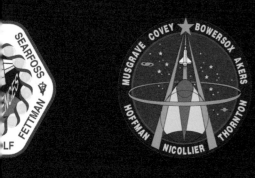

SPACE
MISSION
ART.

THE MISSION PATCHES & INSIGNIAS OF AMERICA'S HUMAN SPACEFLIGHTS

Task Accomplished......
July, 1969

APOLLO 11

NATIONAL AERONAUTICS AND SPACE ADMINISTRATION

SPACE MISSION ART

THE MISSION PATCHES & INSIGNIAS OF AMERICA'S HUMAN SPACEFLIGHTS

LUKE WESLEY PRICE

AMMONITE
PRESS

First published 2019 by
Ammonite Press
an imprint of Guild of Master Craftsman Publications Ltd
Castle Place, 166 High Street, Lewes, East Sussex, BN7 1XU, United Kingdom
www.ammonitepress.com

Text and Design © Luke Wesley Price, 2019
Copyright in the Work © GMC Publications Ltd, 2019
All photographs courtesy of National Aeronautics and
Space Administration (NASA).

ISBN: 978-1-78145-381-0

A catalogue record for this book is available from the British Library.

Publisher: Jason Hook
Design Manager: Robin Shields
Editor: Jamie Pumfrey
Image Research, Editing and Digital Image Processing: Luke Wesley Price

Colour reproduction by GMC Reprographics
Printed and bound in China

Page 2: 24 July 1969 - Flight controllers at NASA's Mission Control Center
in Houston wave their flags in triumph as the crew of Apollo 11 splashdown
safely in the Pacific Ocean upon completion of the first lunar landing.

Page 6: 18 July 2011 - International Space Station crew member Michael
Fossum watches on as STS-135 commander, Christopher Ferguson, applies
the final mission insignia of the Space Shuttle Program to the Space Shuttle
mission-patch wall inside the Unity module of the ISS.

CONTENTS

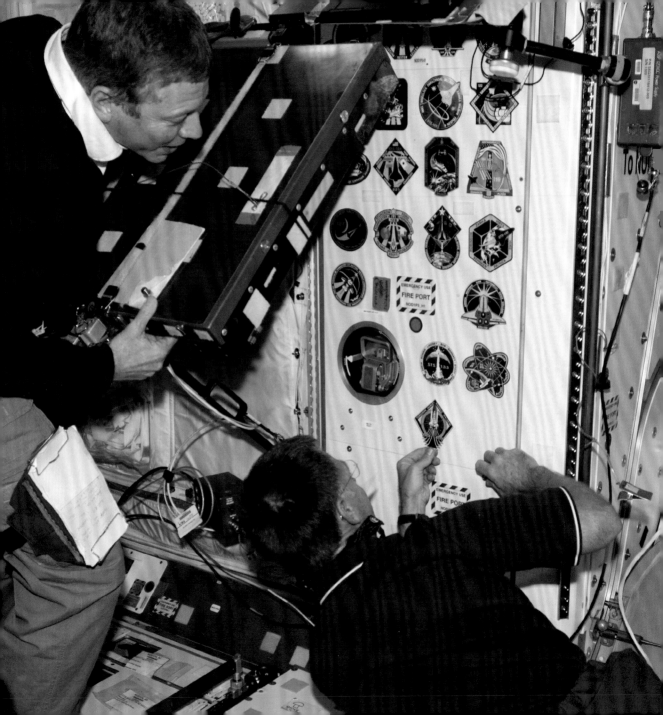

MISSION

Since 1961, the USA has launched men and women into space to extend humankind's knowledge of the universe and discover new horizons. For the adventure on which they were about to embark, astronauts, their family members, co-workers and artists worked tirelessly to commemorate each mission with a bespoke insignia or mission patch that the crew could wear with pride. From Project Mercury through Gemini, Apollo, Skylab, Apollo–Soyuz and up to the Space Shuttle, this book showcases the unique artworks of America's crewed spacecraft and offers insights into the meanings and concepts behind them, all in one visually engaging collection.

As you read through you may notice that mission numbers do not necessarily go in numerical order. This is because missions often got delayed due to technical reasons or equipment/hardware not being ready for launch. Also, you will notice that some missions do not start at number 1 or that some have been omitted. This is because these spaceflights would have been test flights without a human crew.

American astronauts first adopted the use of the custom-designed mission patch on Gemini 5. This collection takes you back even further, to when the original Mercury 7 astronauts decorated the exteriors of their space capsules. Mission patches were often designed by the crews themselves and then developed further by an artist or a group of designers. Sometimes the final design was the result of the combined work of many people and provided the crew with the perfect artwork to reflect their mission. The book contains a brief account of each mission objective, including crew details, to help gain a greater understanding of the story that each insignia is helping to tell. The patches and insignias often contain hidden details and personal symbolic references, and the reader is encouraged to look carefully at the designs and try to uncover some of those elements.

At the back of the book there is a section that lists the known artists, designers and artworkers who contributed to these fine pieces of American space history. Many of them, however, remain unknown and are very likely to have been friends of the crews, family members or employees at NASA art departments. This book pays homage to each and every person who helped to create the mission insignias that provide such a compelling graphic timeline of the American quest to explore space.

PROJECT MERCURY

PROJECT GEMINI

PROJECT APOLLO

SKYLAB

APOLLO-SOYUZ TEST PROJECT

SPACE TRANSPORTATION SYSTEM

INTRODUCTION

My venture into producing space history art books began in 2009 when I decided to combine my profession as a graphic designer with my passion for America's human spaceflight history. After four years of intense research, design and development, I released *Space Shuttle: A Photographic Journey* in a limited first edition of 1981 copies, which quickly became a favourite among space enthusiasts as a definitive tribute to 30 glorious years of the Space Shuttle.

Due to the success of the first edition of *Space Shuttle: A Photographic Journey*, Ammonite Press published a brand new second edition, including a foreword by Christopher Ferguson, three-time Space Shuttle astronaut and commander of the final mission, STS-135. One of the features of the book that people loved was the gallery of mission patches, which led me onto my new project, this book – *Space Mission Art* – a user friendly reference guide to the mission patches and insignias of NASA's human spaceflights.

With a mission to combine interesting historical facts with my passion for elegant design, I proceeded to reach out to astronauts, artists, former NASA graphic designers and other mission patch experts to create a reference guide that is informative, fun for all age groups and visually engaging. NASA holds a wealth of information in its media archives, which was invaluable when creating a project of this scale. The NASA archives served as the backbone of this work, which I have endeavoured to build upon to offer an inspiring insight into each mission and some of the intriguing stories behind the designs of the insignias.

From the first solo American spaceflights of Project Mercury, through to the extensive scientific and ISS assembly missions of the Space Shuttle Program, this book is a tribute to the hard work, relentless training, undeniable courage, dedication and passion of the astronaut crews of NASA's human spaceflights.

Space Mission Art showcases the unique designs those astronauts meticulously created alongside friends, family and artists, to wear with pride and represent their own voyages among the stars.

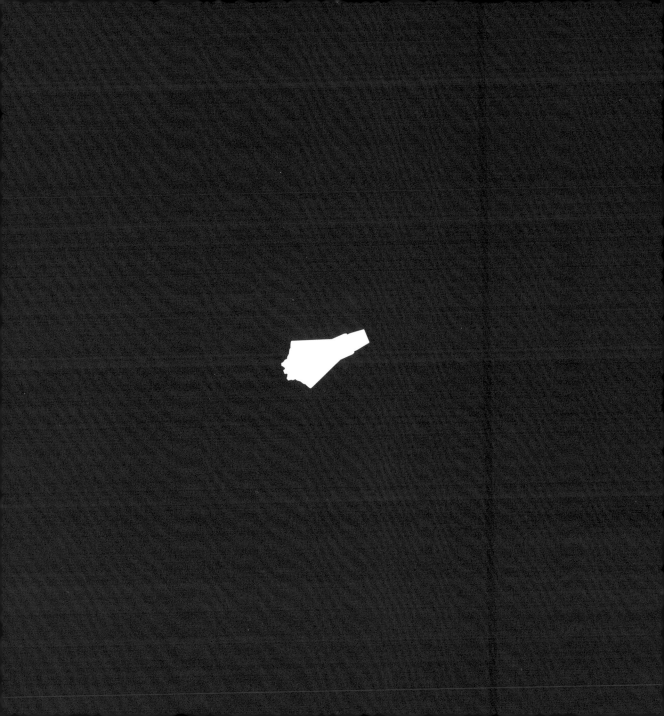

MERCURY

MERCURY-REDSTONE 3

CREW
Alan B. Shepard Jr

SPACECRAFT
Freedom 7
Mercury-Redstone – Rocket/Launch Vehicle

LAUNCH DATE
5 May 1961

MISSION
• First American in space, second human in space.
• 15-minute suborbital spaceflight.

The Mercury 7 astronauts. Left to right (back): Alan Shepard, Gus Grissom, Gordon Cooper; (front): Wally Schirra, Deke Slayton, John Glenn, Scott Carpenter.

Project Mercury was the USA's first human space programme; its goal was to put a man into orbit and return him safely to Earth. It was a period of intense rivalry between the USA and the USSR as to who would dominate the burgeoning space race. In 1957, the Soviets had achieved success by launching the first satellite into orbit with Sputnik 1, and the race was on to launch a human into space. On 12 April 1961, the Soviet spacecraft Vostok 1, carrying cosmonaut Yuri Gagarin, completed one Earth orbit, making Gagarin the first human to leave our world. Three weeks after that historic flight, on 5 May 1961, NASA astronaut Alan B. Shepard became America's first astronaut on board his Mercury spacecraft with a suborbital flight that lasted just over 15 minutes from launch to splashdown. Soon afterwards, President John F. Kennedy made his famous speech to Congress setting out America's goal of 'landing a man on the Moon and returning him safely' by the end of the decade.

Mission patches were not designed throughout Project Mercury and would not be seen until Gemini 5. However, the Mercury astronauts each assigned their spacecraft a name, which was painted onto the exterior of the capsule. Shepard named his Freedom 7. It was the seventh spacecraft off the McDonnell Aircraft Corporation production line, and the Mercury-Redstone rocket was also designated MR-7. Seven astronauts – the Mercury 7 – had the responsibility and honour of piloting America's first voyages into outer space, and consequently all Mercury spacecraft names that followed contained the number 7.

CREW
Virgil I. 'Gus' Grissom

SPACECRAFT
Liberty Bell 7
Mercury-Redstone – Rocket/Launch Vehicle

LAUNCH DATE
21 July 1961

MISSION
• 15-minute suborbital spaceflight.

Astronaut Gus Grissom named his Mercury spacecraft Liberty Bell 7 in homage to the iconic Liberty Bell in Philadelphia, Pennsylvania, a symbol of American independence. The photograph above shows the name marked on the small black Mercury capsule but also a large white crack, which was crudely painted up the side of the bell-shaped spacecraft (partially visible in the image) to represent the famous crack in the Liberty Bell itself.

NASA's second human spaceflight, Mercury-Redstone 4, followed essentially the same flight plan as the first. Grissom's modified Mercury capsule had a larger window in place of the two tiny portholes of Freedom 7, and an explosive hatch was also fitted to allow for a faster exit in an emergency. Grissom experienced approximately five minutes of weightlessness during the suborbital spaceflight, which lasted 15 minutes and 37 seconds.

DID YOU KNOW?

After Liberty Bell 7 had safely splashed down, the newly installed explosive hatch blew prematurely, allowing water to enter the capsule. Grissom then exited the capsule and stayed afloat while awaiting recovery. The flooded spacecraft proved too heavy for the recovery helicopter, and Liberty Bell 7 sank to the bottom of the Atlantic Ocean, where it remained lost for 38 years. It was eventually located and raised from the seabed in 1999.

Gus Grissom climbs into the Liberty Bell 7 on launch day.

CREW

John H. Glenn Jr

SPACECRAFT

Friendship 7
Mercury-Atlas D – Rocket/Launch Vehicle

LAUNCH DATE

20 February 1962

MISSION

• First American to orbit Earth.

Astronaut John Glenn employed the talents of graphic artist Cece Bibby for the design that adorned his Mercury, and the artwork was hand-painted by Bibby directly onto the side of the dull black exterior of the capsule. This custom design expressed a more personal touch than the stencilled names of Freedom 7 and Liberty Bell 7. The word 'friendship' was chosen to reflect America's message to the world during this first orbital spaceflight by NASA.

John Glenn's landmark mission put America on course to continue the pursuit of a lunar landing before the end of the decade. The spaceflight lasted almost five hours, and Glenn completed three orbits before re-entry into Earth's atmosphere.

DID YOU KNOW?

A faulty switch inside John Glenn's Friendship 7 spacecraft falsely indicated that the heat shield may have come loose during the flight, and mission control made the decision to keep the rocket retropack strapped to the shield during re-entry as a precaution. The first American to orbit Earth splashed down safely in the North Atlantic and didn't return to space until his shuttle flight on board STS-95 at the age of 77, becoming the oldest person to date ever to travel into space.

John Glenn lines up the Friendship 7 logo design under the spacecraft's pilot window.

MERCURY-ATLAS

CREW
M. Scott Carpenter

SPACECRAFT
Aurora 7
Mercury-Atlas D – Rocket/Launch Vehicle

LAUNCH DATE
24 May 1962

MISSION
• Three Earth orbits.
• Microgravity experiments and Earth photography.

Scott Carpenter named his Mercury spacecraft Aurora 7, a reference to the scientific objectives of the mission and representing the dawn of a new era in space exploration. Carpenter's flight focused heavily on scientific research and observations of Earth and its weather, and part of the flight plan required him to photograph Earth and atmospheric phenomena. The design featuring the aurora borealis was hand-painted directly onto the craft by graphic artist Cece Bibby (pictured with Carpenter above), who had also designed John Glenn's Friendship 7 logo.

During the mission, NASA became aware that Carpenter was falling behind on his flight-plan checklist and using excessive fuel. The on-board experiments and observational photography were consuming too much of the astronaut's time, and Carpenter fired his retrorockets three seconds late, resulting in Aurora 7 splashing down in the Atlantic Ocean 250 miles (400 kilometres) from the intended landing site. The five-hour Mercury-Atlas 7 mission was Scott Carpenter's only spaceflight.

DID YOU KNOW?
Only six of the Mercury 7 astronauts actually flew into space during Project Mercury. Donald 'Deke' Slayton was originally scheduled to pilot Mercury-Atlas 7 but was diagnosed with a heart condition and grounded. Slayton had planned to name his spacecraft Delta 7.

Scott Carpenter climbs into his Aurora 7 spacecraft on launch day.

MERCURY-ATLAS 8

CREW

Walter M. 'Wally' Schirra Jr

SPACECRAFT

Sigma 7
Mercury-Atlas D – Rocket/Launch Vehicle

LAUNCH DATE

3 October 1962

MISSION

- Six Earth orbits.
- Engineering flight to test and verify upgraded spacecraft systems in preparation for future long-duration flights.

Mercury-Atlas 8 astronaut Wally Schirra named his spacecraft Sigma 7. The red Σ symbol is a Greek letter often used in the fields of engineering and mathematics to mean 'sum', so the name was chosen as a tribute to the countless personnel working across all sectors of the space programme whose collective efforts contributed to the success of the mission. The symbol also reflects the mission's engineering nature. Following on from the two previous spaceflights, Schirra commissioned Cece Bibby to design the insignia, and the photograph above shows her painting the logo onto the spacecraft as Schirra watches on.

The objective of Schirra's flight was to evaluate and verify the capabilities of the Mercury spacecraft itself. Lasting nine hours, this was the longest flight so far, and it was undertaken in preparation for the even longer flight planned for Mercury-Atlas 9 the following year. Schirra piloted the spacecraft with great efficiency and precision, splashing down just four and a half miles (7.25 kilometres) from the intended landing site in the Pacific Ocean. The success of the mission proved the effectiveness of the Mercury in orbital flight and boosted NASA's confidence to press ahead with Project Gemini.

Astronaut Wally Schirra squeezes into his Sigma 7 spacecraft on launch day.

MERCURY-ATLAS 9

CREW

L. Gordon 'Gordo' Cooper Jr

SPACECRAFT

Faith 7
Mercury-Atlas D – Rocket/Launch Vehicle

LAUNCH DATE

15 May 1963

MISSION

• Final spaceflight of Project Mercury.
• 22 Earth orbits lasting over 34 hours in space.
• Last solo American spaceflight.

The final flight of Project Mercury was piloted by Gordon Cooper, who assigned the name Faith 7 to his spacecraft. The name was chosen to symbolize his faith in the craft, in his own abilities to pilot the mission successfully, his faith in the ground crew and his faith in God. As with all previous Mercury insignias, the number 7 represented the Mercury 7 astronauts and the close bond that they had formed.

Cooper's mission lasted 34 hours and completed 22 orbits. Even though the Soviet space programme had already totalled 130 orbits during their four piloted flights, Cooper's exceptional performance on his mission was a significant milestone for NASA, proving they could perform long-duration flights effectively. Towards the end of the flight, the spacecraft's altitude readings and autopilot re-entry systems failed, so Cooper manually piloted the spacecraft and splashed down in the Pacific Ocean just four miles (6.5 kilometres) from the USS *Kearsarge* recovery ship. It was the most precise landing of Project Mercury, and Cooper was welcomed home with a glorious ticker-tape parade that celebrated both his courageous mission and a triumphant completion of Project Mercury.

Gordon Cooper enters his tiny Faith 7 spacecraft prior to launch.

GEMINI

GEMINI

CREW

Virgil I. 'Gus' Grissom – Command Pilot
John W. Young – Pilot

SPACECRAFT

Gemini III (Molly Brown)
Titan II GLV – Rocket/Launch Vehicle

LAUNCH DATE

23 March 1965

MISSION

• First crewed Earth orbital mission of Project
  Gemini to test the new spacecraft.

Left to right: Virgil I. 'Gus' Grissom, John W. Young

Gemini 3 was the first crewed mission of Project Gemini and the second spaceflight for astronaut Gus Grissom. Grissom's first suborbital flight had lasted just over 15 minutes and ended with the Liberty Bell 7 sinking to the bottom of the Atlantic Ocean after the explosive hatch blew and water started to pour into the craft. Grissom and his fellow astronaut John W. Young had named their Gemini spacecraft Molly Brown after the Broadway musical and movie *The Unsinkable Molly Brown*, an adaptation of the life of a lady named Margaret Brown who had survived the sinking of the RMS *Titanic*. The idea of mission patches had not yet been adopted by crew members at this time, but Grissom and Young did carry some souvenir silver medallions on board, and Young was seen often in later years wearing a commemorative Molly Brown mission patch (pictured on his flightsuit above) based on the design of the medallions. This Molly Brown patch is not an official NASA insignia.

The Gemini spacecraft – like the Mercury craft, manufactured by the McDonnell Aircraft Corporation – could accommodate two astronauts and was used to perform new spaceflight techniques, including rendezvous and docking operations, that would be vital in attempting a lunar landing during Project Apollo. The Gemini 3 crew conducted manoeuvring techniques to evaluate the brand-new craft in a flight that lasted 4 hours, 52 minutes and 31 seconds.

GEMINI 4

CREW
James A. McDivitt – Command Pilot
Edward H. White II – Pilot

SPACECRAFT
Gemini IV
Titan II GLV – Rocket/Launch Vehicle

LAUNCH DATE
3 June 1965

MISSION
- Four-day mission to evaluate the effects of longer spaceflights.
- First American spacewalk (EVA) lasting 23 minutes.

Although the adoption of custom-designed mission-specific patches had to wait until Gemini 5, the crew of Gemini 4 started another tradition of their own. Astronauts James McDivitt and Ed White had the Stars and Stripes of the USA sewn onto the left shoulder of their spacesuits, a practice that has been kept by NASA ever since.

Gemini 4 was another important milestone in America's space programme. Astronaut Ed White became the first American to exit a spacecraft and perform a spacewalk attached to a 26¼-foot (8-metre) tether. He used a hand-held gas device to propel himself while outside the craft before relying on the tether to twist and turn while free-floating in space. Cosmonaut Alexei Leonov had already conducted the very first human spacewalk ten weeks earlier on the Soviet Voskhod 2 mission; however, Gemini 4 successfully proved it could be done effectively and was a great step forward for the American programme.

Left to right: James A. McDivitt, Edward H. White II

GEMINI 5

CREW
L. Gordon 'Gordo' Cooper Jr – Command Pilot
Charles 'Pete' Conrad Jr – Pilot

SPACECRAFT
Gemini V
Titan II GLV – Rocket/Launch Vehicle

LAUNCH DATE
21 August 1965

MISSION
- Eight-day mission to evaluate the effects of longer periods in space.
- First use of fuel cells instead of batteries to power the spacecraft.

Left to right: Pete Conrad, Gordon Cooper

It all started here. Gemini 5 was the first American spaceflight to have an official mission patch. Known as the 'Cooper Patch', astronaut Gordon Cooper presented the idea to NASA, who gave the go-ahead. The artwork pays homage to the pioneering nature of NASA's space programme, and features a symbolic reference to the pioneers and settlers of America's westward expansion by depicting a 19th century Conestoga wagon. The design featured the slogan '8 days or bust', but this was ruled against as it could potentially be deemed a failure by the public if the mission fell short of the eight-day objective, the longest mission attempted at that time. Although the patches had already been manufactured, NASA insisted that the '8 days or bust' be covered up. A piece of white cloth was hastily sewn over the slogan for the patches used on the astronaut's spacesuits (inset).

The objectives of Project Gemini were to explore spaceflight techniques and test procedures necessary to attempt a lunar landing, as eight days was the time it would take to travel to the Moon, land and return home. Gemini 5 intended to conduct rendezvous techniques with a Rendezvous Evaluation Pod, but the exercise was aborted after the spacecraft suffered fuel-cell problems. Simulated rendezvous techniques were performed, however, and the mission proved humans could withstand longer periods in space.

DID YOU KNOW?
Veteran astronaut Gordon Cooper retired from NASA in 1970 after failing to secure an Apollo flight. He was the quintessential test-pilot-era astronaut.

GEMINI 7

CREW
Frank F. Borman II – Command Pilot
James A. 'Jim' Lovell Jr – Pilot

SPACECRAFT
Gemini VII
Titan II GLV – Rocket/Launch Vehicle

LAUNCH DATE
4 December 1965

MISSION
• 14-day mission and the first rendezvous in space –
with Gemini 6A – of two crewed spacecraft.

At 14 days, Gemini 7 was to be the longest orbital mission to date, and the mission-patch design showing a hand holding an Olympic-style torch symbolized the duration and endurance objectives of the flight. To the left of the torch is a representation of a Gemini spacecraft, while to the right is VII, number 7 in the Roman numbering system.

Astronauts Frank Borman and Jim Lovell had a series of scientific experiments and other tasks to perform while they were in orbit, including medical experiments and testing what was known as the 'shirtsleeve environment', in which astronauts would perform their duties without wearing a spacesuit. One of the other important objectives of the mission was to rendezvous with a second Gemini spacecraft, Gemini 6A, which launched 11 days after Gemini 7. During the encounter, the two craft flew beside each other, at one point coming as close as one foot (30 centimetres) from one another.

DID YOU KNOW?

Three years after their spaceflight on Gemini 7, Frank Borman and Jim Lovell would once again fly in space together on the legendary Apollo 8 mission. Along with Bill Anders on his first and only spaceflight, they became the first humans to travel to the Moon and enter lunar orbit.

Left to right: Jim Lovell, Frank Borman

GEMINI 6A

Left to right: Tom Stafford, Wally Schirra

The mission patch for Gemini 6A shows two Gemini craft achieving rendezvous in space with the trajectory spelling out the number 6. The Gemini 6A spacecraft (top left) is depicted over two stars, Castor and Pollux, the twin stars of the constellation Gemini. Gemini 7 is shown below, and to its right is the constellation Orion (with Orion's Belt represented by the three small white stars). The patch is hexagonal, and the outer bright-yellow stars form what is known as the Winter Hexagon asterism, a group of six bright stars that make up the six sides of a hexagon. This is relevant to the mission designation, as it was against this stellar backdrop that the rendezvous took place. The stars that make up the Winter Hexagon asterism are Capella (top right), Aldebaran (right), Rigel (bottom right), Sirius (bottom left), Procyon (left) and Pollux (at the top of the Gemini 6A spacecraft). The patch is blue and yellow, most likely in honour of the US services in which Schirra (navy) and Stafford (air force) both served.

Sitting patiently on the launch pad on 25 October 1965, the crew of Gemini 6 was ready for lift-off immediately after the launch of an unpiloted Agena Target Vehicle. The objective had been to achieve the first docking in space. The Agena failed to reach orbit, however, and the Gemini 6 mission was aborted and rescheduled for a later launch date in December. With an updated mission name of Gemini 6A, the crew's new objective was to perform the very first rendezvous in space with another manned craft, Gemini 7, in which Frank Borman and Jim Lovell had launched 11 days earlier on 4 December.

CREW

Neil A. Armstrong – Command Pilot
David R. Scott – Pilot

SPACECRAFT

Gemini VIII
Titan II GLV – Rocket/Launch Vehicle

LAUNCH DATE

16 March 1966

MISSION

• First docking in space with an unpiloted Agena Target Vehicle.

The Gemini 8 mission insignia shows Castor and Pollux, the twin stars of the constellation Gemini. Their light shines through a prism and then separates into the colours of the spectrum to spell out the mission designation using the zodiac symbol for Gemini – which resembles the design used on the official NASA insignia for Project Gemini – followed by the Roman numeral VIII (8). The concept was that Gemini 8 would achieve the full spectrum of tasks intended for Project Gemini: rendezvous techniques, docking in space, extravehicular activity (EVA) and mission experiments, all of which would be used to improve future space missions.

The crew's main objective was to conduct the first piloted docking in space and to rendezvous with an unpiloted Agena Target Vehicle. Armstrong manoeuvred the craft to dock successfully with the Agena six and a half hours after launch, but shortly afterwards the two joined craft began to spin. Armstrong separated from the Agena and eventually managed to gain control of the Gemini. The spinning turned out to have been caused by one of Gemini's thrusters that had been firing continuously, so the mission was cut short and the crew immediately returned to Earth.

DID YOU KNOW?

The Gemini 8 astronauts were the only Gemini crew who both walked on the Moon. Neil Armstrong was the first human to set foot on the lunar surface on Apollo 11 and Dave Scott was the seventh on Apollo 15.

Left to right: Dave Scott, Neil Armstrong

GEMINI 9A

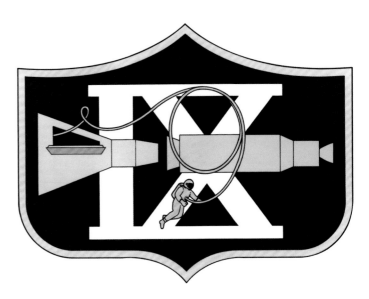

Left to right: Tom Stafford, Gene Cernan

CREW

Thomas P. Stafford – Command Pilot
Eugene A. 'Gene' Cernan – Pilot

SPACECRAFT

Gemini IX-A
Titan II GLV – Rocket/Launch Vehicle

LAUNCH DATE

3 June 1966

MISSION

Rendezvous and planned docking with an unpiloted Augmented Target Docking Adapter (ATDA) after the original Agena Target Vehicle was destroyed during launch.
Flight included a tethered spacewalk.

The Gemini 9A patch illustrates the original mission goals of the previously planned Gemini 9 mission to dock with an Agena Target Vehicle. The design was not altered to show the smaller Augmented Target Docking Adaptor (ATDA) that replaced the Agena when the mission was rescheduled. The large Roman numeral IX (9) in the background is the mission number, and the patch shows an astronaut performing an EVA with the Astronaut Maneuvering Unit (AMU) on his back; the tether depicts the number 9.

Originally scheduled to launch on 17 May 1965, Gemini 9 was cancelled after the Agena Target Vehicle failed to reach orbit earlier that day. NASA launched the ATDA, a smaller docking target, on June 1, and Gemini 9A launched two days later. Once the crew had rendezvoused with the ATDA, they saw that the cover that protected the docking port had failed to separate. Despite this, rendezvous techniques were performed, and Gene Cernan conducted an EVA to test the AMU backpack. However, while trying to retrieve the AMU from its storage space outside at the back of the spacecraft he became fatigued and disorientated, so the EVA was cut short.

DID YOU KNOW?

The original crew for Gemini 9 were Elliot See and Charles Bassett. However, both were killed before their first spaceflight when their NASA T-38 jet crash-landed into the McDonnell Aircraft Corporation facility while on their way to inspect their spacecraft.

CREW

John W. Young – Command Pilot
Michael Collins – Pilot

SPACECRAFT

Gemini X
Titan II GLV – Rocket/Launch Vehicle

LAUNCH DATE

18 July 1966

MISSION

• Rendezvous and docking tests with the unpiloted Agena Target Vehicle.
• Stand-up and tethered spacewalks.

The mission-insignia design for Gemini 10 – created by astronaut John Young's wife at the time, Barbara Young – was worn on the right arm of the crew's spacesuits. A large red Roman X (10) stretches boldly across a blue circle representing Earth, while a silhouetted Gemini spacecraft orbiting the red X can be seen approaching the Agena Target Vehicle, thus symbolizing the rendezvous and docking objectives of the mission. At the centre of the patch are two large yellow stars, Castor and Pollux, the twin stars of the constellation Gemini, which had previously featured on the mission-patch designs for Gemini 6A and Gemini 8.

Gemini 10 was launched into orbit on 18 July 1966, to conduct docking tests with an Agena Target Vehicle. Docking was successful, but too much fuel had been used, so the Gemini stayed attached to the Agena for most of the mission and further tests were aborted. The two craft undocked 39 hours later, and Gemini 10 then rendezvoused with the Agena from the Gemini 8 mission that had taken place three months earlier. Michael Collins performed a tethered spacewalk that including travelling over to the nearby Agena.

DID YOU KNOW?

John Young became one of NASA's most distinguished astronauts after flying into space on Gemini 3, Gemini 10, Apollo 10, Apollo 16 (becoming the ninth man on the Moon), STS-1 (the first shuttle spaceflight) and STS-9.

Left to right: John Young, Michael Collins

GEMINI 11

CREW

Charles 'Pete' Conrad Jr – Command Pilot
Richard F. 'Dick' Gordon Jr – Pilot

SPACECRAFT

Gemini XI
Titan II GLV – Rocket/Launch Vehicle

LAUNCH DATE

12 September 1966

MISSION

- First-orbit rendezvous and docking tests with the unpiloted Agena Target Vehicle.
- Highest Earth-orbital altitude.

Left to right: Dick Gordon, Pete Conrad

The Gemini 11 insignia uses the blue and gold of the US Navy in honour of the crew's backgrounds in that service. The Roman numeral XI (11) soars from the launch site at Cape Kennedy, Florida, and we see the trajectory of the Gemini spacecraft and Agena Target Vehicle that was launched the same day. If you follow the flight path around, you reach a small yellow star that marks the first-orbit rendezvous point of the two craft. Follow the path further, and Gemini 11 can be seen docking with the Agena, symbolized by a white star. The flight path then reaches the top of the patch, representing the high-altitude target of the mission, marked by another white star. As the flight path drops towards the right-hand side, an astronaut can be seen performing a tethered spacewalk with another white star underneath him indicating the fourth mission milestone.

The mission objective for Gemini 11 was to achieve a first-orbit rendezvous and docking between two spacecraft. This was to help simulate techniques that would be employed in future Apollo missions when the Lunar Module would rendezvous with the Command and Service Module in lunar orbit. Dick Gordon performed both stand-up and tethered spacewalks during the flight.

DID YOU KNOW?

Gemini 11 achieved the highest Earth orbital altitude of any other mission. The crew used the engine of the attached Agena to boost their altitude to a staggering 853 miles (1,373 kilometres) above Earth.

CREW

James A. 'Jim' Lovell Jr – Command Pilot
Edwin E. 'Buzz' Aldrin Jr – Pilot

SPACECRAFT

Gemini XII
Titan II GLV – Rocket/Launch Vehicle

LAUNCH DATE

11 November 1966

MISSION

- Final spaceflight of Project Gemini.
- Rendezvous and docking tests with the unpiloted Agena Target Vehicle.
- Stand-up and tethered spacewalks.

The Gemini 12 insignia is a simple yet very effective design. The centre of the patch illustrates a Gemini spacecraft in its upright position pointing to the Roman numeral XII (12), suggesting a clock face and symbolizing both the mission number and the final hour of Project Gemini. The mission also coincided with the total solar eclipse of 12 November 1966, and this is referenced in the design with the black portion representing the Moon in front of the yellow of the Sun on the left. The crescent has also been thought to stand for the Moon and flagging the upcoming Apollo lunar missions and the significant role Project Gemini played in making those possible. The black and orange is also a nod to Halloween or 31 October, which was the original planned launch date. Anthony Tharenos, an ex-McDonnell Aircraft graphic designer, created the final artwork for the patch with creative guidance from the crew.

Gemini 12 was the tenth crewed mission and final flight of Project Gemini. After docking with the Agena Target Vehicle, which had been launched earlier that same morning, Gemini 12 witnessed and photographed the total solar eclipse. The crew had 14 on-board experiments consisting of medical, scientific and technological research. Buzz Aldrin carried out two stand-up EVAs and one tethered, proving that astronauts could operate and perform tasks effectively outside the spacecraft. Splashdown of the last Gemini mission occurred in the Atlantic Ocean on 15 November 1966, bringing that chapter of space exploration to an end and marking the start of a new one, Project Apollo, and the goal of landing a man on the Moon and returning him safely to Earth before the end of the 1960s.

Left to right: Buzz Aldrin, Jim Lovell

APOLLO

APOLLO 1

CREW
Virgil I. 'Gus' Grissom – Command Pilot
Edward H. White II – Senior Pilot
Roger B. Chaffee – Pilot

SPACECRAFT
CSM-012 – Command and Service Module
Saturn 1B, AS-204 – Rocket/Launch Vehicle

LAUNCH DATE
21 February 1967 (planned launch date). Crew perished during preflight test, 27 January 1967.

MISSION
- First scheduled crewed test flight of the Apollo Command and Service Module.
- Fire on the launch pad resulted in the death of the crew.

Left to right: Virgil 'Gus' Grissom , Ed White, Roger Chaffee

With the Stars and Stripes used as a border, the Apollo 1 mission patch shows the Apollo Command and Service Module flying over the launch site at Cape Kennedy, Florida. The Moon is in the distance, symbolizing the ultimate goal of Project Apollo. The designer was Allen Stevens of North American Aviation, manufacturer of the Command and Service Module.

On 27 January 1967, the crew of Apollo 1 – Gus Grissom, Ed White and Roger Chaffee – were tragically killed during a preflight test on the launch pad. They were strapped inside and all cables supplying power while on the ground removed, allowing the spacecraft to run on its own power to simulate a real launch. Tragically, a spark caused a deadly fire inside the highly pressurized capsule, which, crucially, was filled with pure oxygen, and this contributed to the rapid spread of the conflagration that the crew were unable to escape. Later missions used a different, less volatile, mix of gases, and more efficient outwards-opening hatches were designed to allow for a quicker escape from the Command Module in an any future emergency.

DID YOU KNOW?
Materials that were discovered to be highly flammable in a pure-oxygen environment were deemed to be a significant factor in the rapid spread of the fire. The tragedy caused NASA to rethink and redesign many elements of the spacecraft and the astronauts' suits, including the use of self-extinguishing and melt-resisting materials. All future ground tests and launch procedures would be done in a mixed nitrogen-and-oxygen environment.

The Apollo 7 mission patch – created by artist Allen Stevens – shows the Command and Service Module's orbit around Earth represented by the rocket's trail. The mission's designated number is shown in Roman numerals over the Pacific Ocean with North and South America and the Florida launch site of Project Apollo sitting underneath the craft.

After the tragic Apollo 1 fire, the next mission to carry a crew was Apollo 7 in October 1968 – the intervening Apollo launches were a series of unpiloted test flights. The mission lasted 11 days and would test the flight characteristics of the Command and Service Module while also broadcasting the first live television stream from an American space mission. During the flight, the crew all suffered from severe colds that had developed while in space. Against NASA's advice, they decided to keep their helmets off during re-entry; they would not have been able to blow their noses with their helmets on, and they were concerned that too much pressure might build up in their heads if they were unable to do so.

DID YOU KNOW?

Wally Schirra is the only astronaut to have flown into space on all American spaceflight programmes up to Project Apollo. He was the fifth American to fly into space on Project Mercury (MA-8), was on the fifth human flight for Project Gemini (Gemini 6A) and was commander of the first Apollo mission into space with Apollo 7.

APOLLO 7

CREW

Walter M. 'Wally' Schirra Jr – Commander
Donn F. Eisele – Command Module Pilot
R. Walter Cunningham – Lunar Module Pilot

SPACECRAFT

CSM-101 – Command and Service Module
Saturn 1B, AS-205 – Rocket/Launch Vehicle

LAUNCH DATE

11 October 1968

MISSION

• First crewed Apollo mission to test the Command and Service Module in space.

Left to right: Donn Eisele, Wally Schirra, Walter Cunningham

APOLLO 8

CREW
Frank F. Borman II – Commander
James A. 'Jim' Lovell Jr – Command Module Pilot
William A. 'Bill' Anders – Lunar Module Pilot

SPACECRAFT
CSM-103 – Command and Service Module
Saturn V, AS-503 – Rocket/Launch Vehicle

LAUNCH DATE
21 December 1968

MISSION
First crewed flight to the Moon and first lunar orbit.

Left to right: Jim Lovell, Bill Anders, Frank Borman

The Apollo 8 patch was originally conceived by astronaut Jim Lovell and designed by artist William Bradley. The shape of this iconic design resembles the Command Module, and the red 8 represents the mission number while also signifying the trajectory of the mission to the Moon and back.

Apollo 8 was a true landmark in space history. Following the successful flight of Apollo 7, Apollo 8 was originally intended to be a second low-Earth-orbit flight during which the crew would carry out the first flight-characteristic tests of the Lunar Module. Because of a delay in the Lunar Module being ready for flight, the mission was changed to make it the first lunar orbit. Astronauts Jim Lovell, Frank Borman and Bill Anders would now become the first humans to leave Earth's orbit, the first to reach and orbit the Moon, the first to view Earth in its entirety with their own eyes and the first to spend Christmas in space. They were also the first crew to be launched by the mighty Saturn V rocket.

DID YOU KNOW?
As the crew of Apollo 8 reappeared from the far side of the Moon on Christmas Eve, 1968, they witnessed Earth rising in the distance over the Moon's horizon. Bill Anders grabbed a Hasselblad camera and shot the iconic Earthrise image. It was the first colour photograph of Earth in its entirety taken by a human in space.

APOLLO

CREW

James A. McDivitt – Commander
David R. Scott – Command Module Pilot
Russell L. 'Rusty' Schweickart – Lunar Module Pilot

SPACECRAFT

Gumdrop, CSM-104 – Command and Service Module
Spider, LM-3 – Lunar Module
Saturn V, AS-504 – Rocket/Launch Vehicle

LAUNCH DATE

3 March 1969

MISSION

- First crewed test flight of the Lunar Module in Earth orbit.
- First mission to take a complete Apollo spacecraft into space.

The Apollo 9 insignia illustrates all elements of the entire spacecraft: the Saturn V rocket (left) and the Command and Service Module, its orbit around Earth represented by a yellow trail, rendezvousing with the Lunar Module. The red-filled D signifies that Apollo 9 was a 'D' mission – a human spaceflight undertaken primarily to test the performance of the Lunar Module. The artist was Allen Stevens of North American Rockwell (previously North American Aviation), the prime contractor for the Apollo Command and Service Module.

The crew of Apollo 9 was the first to take the spidery Lunar Module for a test flight. It was a crude-looking craft, but it would eventually carry two astronauts to the lunar surface and keep them safe throughout their mission. The module itself was comprised of two parts, the descent stage, with its iconic golden legs and storage compartment, that descended to the surface, and the ascent stage. After lunar-surface exploration was completed, the ascent stage blasted off to rendezvous with the Command and Service Module leaving the descent stage permanently on the Moon. Once the crew was back on board the Command and Service Module, the ascent stage was jettisoned into lunar orbit and left to crash into the Moon's surface.

DID YOU KNOW?

The Apollo 9 crew was the first to name their spacecraft. The Command Module was called Gumdrop because of its shape and the Lunar Module was, appropriately, named Spider.

Left to right: James McDivitt, David Scott, Rusty Schweickart

CREW

Thomas P. Stafford – Commander
John W. Young – Command Module Pilot
Eugene A. 'Gene' Cernan – Lunar Module Pilot

SPACECRAFT

Charlie Brown, CSM-106 – Command and Service Module
Snoopy, LM-4 – Lunar Module
Saturn V, AS-505 – Rocket/Launch Vehicle

LAUNCH DATE

18 May 1969

MISSION

• First lunar-orbital test flight of the Lunar Module.
• Descent towards the lunar surface without the landing.
• Test run to prepare for the first Moon landing.

Left to right: Gene Cernan, John Young, Thomas Stafford

Thomas Stafford and Gene Cernan had flown together on Gemini 9A, and the mission-patch design for Apollo 10 shows similarities to their Gemini design. In the centre is a large Roman numeral X (10) with the Command and Service Module flying through the upper section. The ascent stage of the Lunar Module is seen flying low over the lunar surface before it docks with the orbiting Command and Service Module. Even though Apollo 10 would not make a lunar landing, the large X is shown sitting firmly on the surface, representing the mission's contribution to reaching the Moon. Earth is present in the background with North and South America visible. Artist Allen Stevens designed the insignia with guidance from the crew.

Apollo 10 was a dress rehearsal for a lunar landing attempt by Apollo 11, and the crew would do everything apart from actually land on the surface. They orbited the Moon in the Lunar Module and descended to approximately eight miles (13 kilometres) above the surface to test its flight characteristics in lunar orbit. The mission lasted eight days, and the astronauts were the first to broadcast in colour from space. After they had completed their flight of the Lunar Module, the ascent stage was jettisoned and the engine fired until fuel depletion, setting it on a course to orbit the Sun.

DID YOU KNOW?

Gene Cernan got another opportunity to return to the Moon as mission commander of Apollo 17. This time, however, he walked on the lunar surface and would eventually be known as the 'last man on the moon'.

APOLLO 11

CREW

Neil A. Armstrong – Commander
Michael Collins – Command Module Pilot
Edwin E. 'Buzz' Aldrin Jr – Lunar Module Pilot

SPACECRAFT

Columbia, CSM-107 – Command and Service Modul
Eagle, LM-5 – Lunar Module
Saturn V, AS-506 – Rocket/Launch Vehicle

LAUNCH DATE

16 July 1969

MISSION

• First humans to land and walk on the Moon.

Originally sketched by Command Module Pilot Michael Collins, the Apollo 11 mission patch shows a bald eagle – a classic symbol of the USA, in honour of their Lunar Module named Eagle – swooping down to land on the Moon while holding an olive branch in its talons to represent the peaceful nature of the mission. The olive branch had originally been in the eagle's beak, but NASA deemed the open talons to be too aggressive. The Earth is shown in the background, but there are no stars illustrated as they would not be visible while standing on the Moon. The crew opted to leave their names off the design as they felt the mission was not just about them and that it was an achievement for all who had worked on the project. The final design of the insignia was created by artist Jim Cooper.

Apollo 11 was the first time humans had set foot on another world. Mission commander Neil Armstrong was the first, with Lunar Module pilot Buzz Aldrin following down the steps of the Lunar Module about 20 minutes later. They planted the Stars and Stripes into the lunar soil on 21 July 1969, fulfilling the goal set by President John F. Kennedy eight years earlier. The two astronauts spent just over two and a half hours on the Moon, setting up experiments, collecting samples and taking extensive photographs.

DID YOU KNOW?

Neil Armstrong spoke his famous words as he stepped onto the lunar surface: 'That's one small step for man, one giant leap for mankind.'

Left to right: Neil Armstrong, Michael Collins, Buzz Aldrin

CREW

Charles 'Pete' Conrad Jr – Commander
Richard F. 'Dick' Gordon Jr – Command Module Pilot
Alan L. Bean – Lunar Module Pilot

SPACECRAFT

Yankee Clipper, CSM-108 – Command and Service
Module
Intrepid, LM-6 – Lunar Module
Saturn V, AS-507 – Rocket/Launch Vehicle

LAUNCH DATE

14 November 1969

MISSION

• Second lunar landing.
• Extensive lunar exploration and scientific experiments.

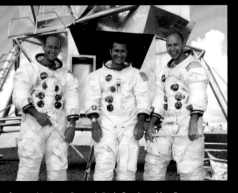

Left to right: Pete Conrad, Dick Gordon, Alan Bean

Employing the US Navy colours of blue and gold, the Apollo 12 mission patch – created by artist Victor Craft – shows a clipper ship racing towards the Moon, flying the Stars and Stripes from its mast. This signified the naval background of the crew and acknowledged the key role clippers had played in discovering new lands on Earth, just as the Apollo spacecraft was taking humans to new worlds. The Moon's Ocean of Storms, the landing site for Apollo 12, can be seen on the left. Four bright stars are depicted, one for each of the crew and one for Clifton C. 'CC' Williams, the original Lunar Module pilot for Apollo 12. Williams was tragically killed in 1967 when his NASA T-38 crashed.

When commander Pete Conrad exited the Lunar Module and stepped onto lunar soil his first words were, 'Whoopie! Man, that may have been a small one for Neil, but that's a long one for me.' Conrad had a reputation for being one of the more playful astronauts, and this historic moment was no different. The crew performed two walks on the Moon, each lasting nearly four hours, collecting samples and setting up experiments. They carried a colour TV camera on board, but while Alan Bean was setting it up, he inadvertently pointed it in the direction of the Sun, rendering it useless.

DID YOU KNOW?

The exuberant crew of Apollo 12 all had custom gold-and-black 1969 Chevrolet Corvette Stingrays. Each had his mission title on the side of their car: CDR for Conrad, LMP for Bean and CMP for Gordon.

CREW

James A. 'Jim' Lovell Jr – Commander
John L. 'Jack' Swigert Jr – Command Module Pilot
Fred W. Haise Jr – Lunar Module Pilot

SPACECRAFT

Odyssey, CSM-109 – Command and Service Module
Aquarius, LM-7 – Lunar Module
Saturn V, AS-508 – Rocket/Launch Vehicle

LAUNCH DATE

11 April 1970

MISSION

• Aborted third attempt at landing on the Moon.

The Apollo 13 patch was initially conceived by artist Lumen Winter with final artwork by Norman Tiller, who placed his initials on one of the horses' legs. It features three golden horses racing towards the Moon from Earth. These are the horses that pull the chariot of Apollo, the Greek Sun god, who is represented by a blazing Sun shining over Earth and the Moon to symbolize the knowledge that Project Apollo has brought to humankind – the Latin phrase 'Ex luna, scientia' translates as 'From the Moon, knowledge'.

During day three of the mission, approximately 200,000 miles (320,000 kilometres) from home, an oxygen tank exploded, causing major damage to the spacecraft and potential catastrophe for the crew as life-support systems began to fail and oxygen was rapidly venting into space. The Command and Service Module was shut down to conserve power, and the crew used the Lunar Module as a lifeboat for the duration of their journey. Having performed a slingshot around the Moon, when they reached Earth orbit the crew climbed back into the crippled Command and Service Module and powered it up for their descent. The mission was classified as a 'Successful Failure' because of the intense work carried out by the crew and personnel at mission control to get the three astronauts home safely.

DID YOU KNOW?

Jim Lovell had already been to the Moon on Apollo 8, but after the explosion his dream of walking on the lunar surface was over. It was Lovell who famously spoke the words, 'Houston, we've had a problem.'

Left to right: Jim Lovell, Jack Swigert, Fred Haise

CREW

Alan B. Shepard Jr – Commander
Stuart A. Roosa – Command Module Pilot
Edgar D. Mitchell – Lunar Module Pilot

SPACECRAFT

Kitty Hawk, CSM-110 – Command and Service Module
Antares, LM-8 – Lunar Module
Saturn V, AS-509 – Rocket/Launch Vehicle

LAUNCH DATE

31 January 1971

MISSION

- Precision landing mission at Fra Mauro, the intended landing site of Apollo 13.
- Two-day stay on the Moon consisting of further scientific experiments, geological investigations and extensive photography.

Left to right: Stuart Roosa, Alan Shepard, Edgar Mitchell

The Apollo 14 mission patch – designed by graphic artist Jean Bealieu – depicts a gold astronaut lapel pin blasting off from Earth and leaving a trail behind on its way to the Moon. The gold badge was worn only by those who had flown in space; a silver version was awarded to astronauts who had yet to complete a spaceflight.

After the failed landing attempt of Apollo 13, the crew of Apollo 14 would now explore the Moon's Fra Mauro crater region, the intended landing site of Apollo 13. Apollo 14 was designated an 'H' mission, as were Apollos 12 and 13. These were precision-landing missions with a maximum stay of two days and two scheduled EVAs. After the landings of Apollos 11 and 12, red stripes were added to the mission commander's spacesuit and helmet for all future landings. This was so mission control back on Earth could better identify each individual astronaut while they were undertaking an EVA. Jim Lovell's Apollo 13 suit had also featured the stripes, but Apollo 14 was the first time the device was used to effect on the lunar surface.

DID YOU KNOW?

Mission commander Alan Shepard became the first American in space, experiencing microgravity for just a few minutes during his 15-minute suborbital flight in 1961. He was the only Mercury 7 astronaut to set foot on the lunar surface and the only human to have played golf on the moon.

APOLLO 15

CREW

David R. Scott – Commander
Alfred M. Worden – Command Module Pilot
James B. 'Jim' Irwin – Lunar Module Pilot

SPACECRAFT

Endeavour, CSM-112 – Command and Service Module
Falcon, LM-10 – Lunar Module
Saturn V, AS-510 – Rocket/Launch Vehicle

LAUNCH DATE

26 July 1971

MISSION

• Extended duration on the lunar surface, including use of the first Lunar Roving Vehicle.

The concept for the Apollo 15 insignia was originally conceived by fashion designer Emilio Pucci, with artwork produced by artist Jerry Elmore. The patch shows three symbols representing flight, one for each of the crew. In the background we can see the Hadley-Apennine landing site of the mission, while to the right of the three symbols the Roman numeral XV (15) can be seen, almost hidden in the shadows of the craters on the lunar surface. Back on Earth, the astronauts all drove customized Chevrolet Corvette Stingrays: Al Worden's was white, Dave Scott's was blue and Jim Irwin's was red, matching the colours used here.

Apollo 15 was the first of the 'J' missions, which were extended stays on the lunar surface with a greater emphasis on exploration and scientific experimentation. The crew of Apollo 15 was the first to drive a vehicle on the Moon; the Lunar Roving Vehicle allowed the astronauts to explore further afield than previous missions. During the flight, Command Module pilot Al Worden was the first person to conduct a spacewalk in deep space.

DID YOU KNOW?

Dave Scott performed an experiment for the TV cameras while on the Moon. He held a hammer in one hand and a falcon feather in the other – in honour of their Lunar Module, Falcon – and dropped them at the same time. Because of the lack of atmosphere, both items landed simultaneously, confirming Galileo's theory that objects will fall at the same rate in a vacuum, regardless of their weight.

Left to right: Jim Irwin, Dave Scott, Al Worden

APOLLO 16

CREW

John W. Young – Commander
Thomas K. 'Ken' Mattingly II – Command Module Pilot
Charles M. Duke Jr – Lunar Module Pilot

SPACECRAFT

Casper, CSM-113 – Command and Service Module
Orion, LM-11 – Lunar Module
Saturn V, AS-511 – Rocket/Launch Vehicle

LAUNCH DATE

16 April 1972

MISSION

- The second 'J' mission, settling down in the lunar highlands.
- Further experiments on the surface, including extensive sample collection and exploration in the Lunar Roving Vehicle.

Left to right: Ken Mattingly, John Young, Charlie Duke

The insignia design for Apollo 16 – created by graphic designer Barbara Matelski – features 16 stars around the edge and the astronauts' names at the bottom. Set against the backdrop of the lunar surface, a bald eagle sits on top of a shield that represents the flag of the USA and its people. The golden 'wing' across the centre of the patch is that used on the NASA logo and is intended to acknowledge the extensive contributions from everyone involved at the agency.

The crew spent nearly three days on the lunar surface, and the entire mission lasted 11 days. The objectives were to survey and collect samples from the lunar highlands. Command Module pilot Ken Mattingly was originally on the primary crew for Apollo 13; however, three days before the launch, he was removed from the mission after having been exposed to German measles and replaced by Jack Swigert. He never contracted the virus and was later assigned to be Command Module pilot for Apollo 16. During the return flight, Mattingly conducted an EVA to retrieve photographic film from a storage area outside the spacecraft.

DID YOU KNOW?

Nine years after this historic flight, John Young became the first astronaut to pilot the Space Shuttle on its maiden voyage into space in 1981.

CREW

Eugene A. 'Gene' Cernan – Commander
Ronald E. Evans – Command Module Pilot
Harrison H. 'Jack' Schmitt – Lunar Module Pilot

SPACECRAFT

America, CSM-114 – Command and Service Module
Challenger, LM-12 – Lunar Module
Saturn V, AS-512 – Rocket/Launch Vehicle

LAUNCH DATE

7 December 1972

MISSION

• The final Apollo mission to the Moon, consisting of extended scientific experimentation and geological surveys of the Taurus-Littrow valley.

The Apollo 17 patch was designed by renowned space artist Robert McCall. The artwork depicts the Greek god Apollo looking towards distant planets and stars, indicating the future of space exploration. Behind Apollo is a bald eagle with the red stripes of the US flag and three stars to represent the crew. The eagle's wing touches the lunar surface to mark the human presence on the Moon, while the golds are used to communicate the golden era of human space exploration.

Apollo 17 was the final crewed flight to the Moon, making mission commander Gene Cernan the last man to walk on the lunar surface to date. The crew conducted extensive scientific and geological exploration with the Lunar Roving Vehicle and, at 75 hours, spent the longest amount of time on the lunar surface of any mission, carrying out three Moon walks, each of which lasted more than seven hours.

DID YOU KNOW?

Astronaut Harrison 'Jack' Schmitt was the first professional scientist to venture into space. Originally a geologist, Schmitt was the first astronaut not to be from a military or test-pilot background and is the only professional scientist ever to have walked on the Moon.

Left to right: Jack Schmitt, Gene Cernan, Ron Evans

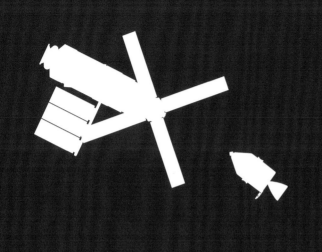

SKYLAB / APOLLO-SOYUZ

CREW

Charles 'Pete' Conrad Jr – Commander
Paul J. Weitz – Pilot
Joseph P. Kerwin – Science Pilot

SPACECRAFT

CSM-116 – Command and Service Module
Saturn 1B, AS-206 – Rocket/Launch Vehicle

LAUNCH DATE

25 May 1973

MISSION

- 28-day mission aboard Skylab to study the effects on humans of spending longer periods in space.
- Emergency repairs to the damaged space station.

Left to right: Joseph Kerwin, Pete Conrad, Paul Weitz

The mission patches for the Skylab project were met with some confusion during their design-and-production phase, and the artwork for all three crewed flights display the incorrect official mission numbers. Originally, the crews adopted the 1-2-3 approach for their designs, as they would be the first three human missions; however, NASA decided to refer to the unpiloted launch of the Skylab space station as Skylab 1. Time constraints meant the patches were not altered, and they adorned the spacesuits and flightsuits, most of which were already stored aboard Skylab in preparation for the crew's subsequent arrival. The Skylab 2 patch shows the silhouetted space station witnessing a solar eclipse as Earth moves in front of the Sun; the Command and Service Module can be seen docked with the space station. The artwork was produced by science-fiction and fantasy artist Kelly Freas.

Skylab, a revolutionary scientific space station and the next step in advancing human presence in space, was launched without a crew on 14 May 1973. As well as vast scientific, medical and astronomical experiments, a primary goal was to study how humans cope and perform in a microgravity environment for extended periods of time. During launch, a thermal protective shield ripped off, making the station uninhabitable, and one of the solar power panels was destroyed while the other only partially deployed. Skylab 2 launched on 25 May carrying a thermal parasol which was deployed over the damaged section, and the jammed solar panel was released during one of three spacewalks. Temperatures dropped, and Skylab was back on track.

CREW

Alan L. Bean – Commander
Jack R. Lousma – Pilot
Owen K. Garriott – Science Pilot

SPACECRAFT

CSM-117 – Command and Service Module
Saturn 1B, AS-207 – Rocket/Launch Vehicle

LAUNCH DATE

28 July 1973

MISSION

- 59-day mission on board Skylab to study the effects on the human body of long periods in space.
- Scientific studies of Earth and the Sun.

The Skylab 3 insignia – marked as Skylab 2 – focuses on the three major objectives of the mission: medical studies of the human body and the effects of living in a weightless environment, study of the Sun and solar activity and to survey Earth and its natural resources. The human figure is an adaptation of Leonardo da Vinci's artwork titled *The Vitruvian Man*, a drawing that shows the idealized proportions of the human body. The left hemisphere illustrates the Sun coloured red (as it could be seen from the Apollo Telescopic Mount attached to Skylab) and the orange solar flare is reminiscent of one that crew member Owen Garriott studied earlier in his career. The hemisphere to the right shows Earth, focusing on North and South America, with the USA represented by the red, white and blue colour scheme.

Skylab 3 was the second and final spaceflight for astronaut Alan Bean, the fourth man on the Moon. During the course of the mission a more substantial thermal parasol was installed over the existing one that had been deployed by the crew of Skylab 2. As well as three spacewalks, Skylab 3's crew fulfilled an extensive range of scientific experiments throughout a mission that lasted 59 days and made 858 Earth orbits.

Left to right: Owen Garriott, Jack Lousma, Alan Bean

SKYLAB 4

CREW

Gerald P. Carr – Commander
William R. Pogue – Pilot
Edward G. Gibson – Science Pilot

SPACECRAFT

CSM-118 – Command and Service Module
Saturn 1B, AS-208 – Rocket/Launch Vehicle

LAUNCH DATE

16 November 1973

MISSION

- Final mission to Skylab, lasting 84 days.
- Observation of the comet Kohoutek.
- Scientific and medical experiments studying the effects on the human body from long periods in space.

Left to right: Gerald Carr, Edward Gibson, William Pogue

The three icons in the Skylab 4 design – created by graphic artist Barbara Matelski – represent the three main objectives of the mission: the human silhouette references the medical studies on the human body during the course of the mission; the tree is an emblem of the study of Earth and its natural resources; and the hydrogen atom, the most abundant element in space, symbolizes the formation of the universe, human exploration of Earth, the implementation of knowledge and the development of technology. Extensive solar observations were carried out during this mission, so the hydrogen atom is appropriate because hydrogen is the primary element of the Sun. The rainbow is a sign of peace and is portrayed embracing humanity (it is also a reference to the biblical story of Noah and the flood), and it curves towards the tree and the hydrogen atom, uniting all three and making a statement as to how important it is that human technological advances are not at the expense of an imbalance between human activities and nature.

Skylab 4 was the final mission to the space station, and it was the only spaceflight for crew members Carr, Pogue and Gibson, albeit a long and exhausting one. Skylab remained uninhabited, orbiting Earth until it broke up in Earth's atmosphere on 11 July 1979.

CREW

Thomas P. Stafford – Commander
Vance D. Brand – Command Module Pilot
Donald K. 'Deke' Slayton – Docking Pilot
Alexey A. Leonov – Commander
Valeri N. Kubasov – Flight Engineer

SPACECRAFT

CSM-111 – Command and Service Module
Saturn 1B, AS-210 – Rocket/Launch Vehicle
Soyuz 19 – Spacecraft/Capsule
Soyuz-U – Rocket/Launch Vehicle

LAUNCH DATE

15 July 1975

MISSION

• First docking in space between two spacecraft from different nations – the USA and USSR.

The mission patch for the Apollo–Soyuz Test Project was originally designed by Jean Pinataro of North American Rockwell, the contractor who built the Apollo Command and Service Module. The artwork went through a series of changes before finally settling on the classic design above. The central illustration took inspiration from a painting by artist Robert McCall who had previously designed the Apollo 17 patch. The image commemorates the first international docking in space and depicts the Soviet Soyuz 19 spacecraft rendezvousing with the American Apollo craft, complete with a specially designed docking module installed. The blazing sun overhead is an emblem of the unity of both nations on this historic flight and of the bright future for international cooperation in space. The left-hand side of the patch and the three white stars represent the American crew; the right-hand side displays the word Soyuz along with the two cosmonauts' names and two stars. The word 'soyuz' translates into English as 'union', a fitting term to mark the first international collaboration in space.

DID YOU KNOW?

Donald 'Deke' Slayton was one of the original Mercury 7 astronauts selected by NASA in 1959. He was grounded in 1962 after being diagnosed with a heart condition, and in 1963 was assigned the role of Director of Flight Crew Operations at NASA. Slayton returned to full flight status in 1972 and made his first and only spaceflight on the Apollo–Soyuz Test Project in 1975.

Left to right: Slayton, Stafford, Brand, Leonov and Kubasov. All are wearing the official insignia, but both crews wore the mission patch. The cosmonauts also wore a Soviet patch.

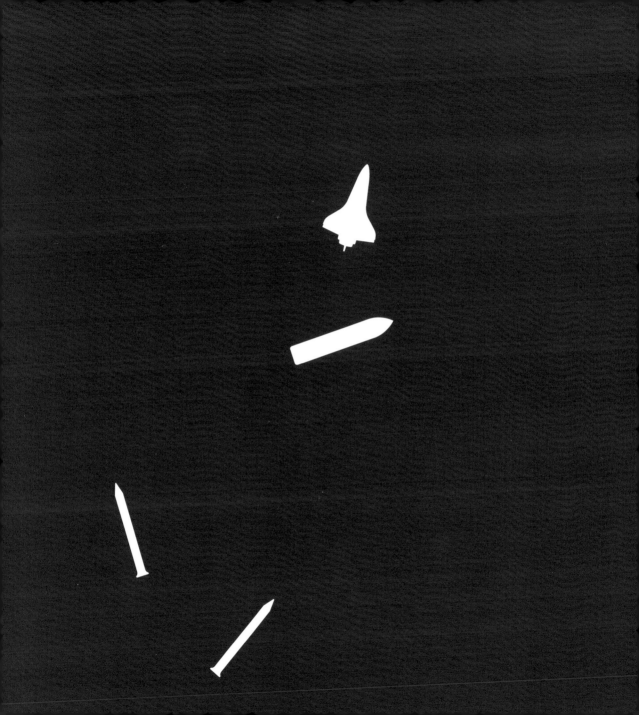

SPACE SHUTTLE

STS-1

CREW

John W. Young – Commander
Robert L. 'Bob' Crippen – Pilot

SPACECRAFT

Columbia, OV-102

LAUNCH DATE

12 April 1981

MISSION

• First orbital spaceflight of the Space Shuttle Columbia.
• Test-flight mission lasting two days and six hours.

Left to right: John Young, Bob Crippen

The artwork of this iconic insignia was created by space artist Robert McCall. It shows the shuttle blasting off, with the orbiter's name, Columbia, in large blue letters above the names of the two crew members. In the background is Earth with a smaller shuttle circling it and leaving a red trail, representing the orbital nature of all shuttle missions and the beginning of a brand-new and exciting era in space exploration.

The Space Transportation System (STS), more commonly known as the Space Shuttle Program, began when STS-1 went into orbit in April 1981. John Young and Bob Crippen put the orbiter vehicle through its paces for two days, testing flight characteristics, carrying out system checks and verifying the performance of whole spacecraft, including the two solid rocket boosters and the external fuel tank. Prior to this, no crewed spacecraft could be reused, but the shuttle was developed as a vehicle that could be flown into space time and time again, making it a uniquely valuable asset for space exploration and establishing a more permanent human presence in space with the construction of the International Space Station.

DID YOU KNOW?

Already a highly distinguished astronaut after two Gemini and two Apollo flights, including a lunar landing on Apollo 16, John Young had the honour and responsibility of taking the shuttle on its maiden orbital flight. He commanded two shuttle missions, STS-1 and STS-9, his final spaceflight.

CREW

Joe H. Engle – Commander
Richard H. 'Dick' Truly – Pilot

SPACECRAFT

Columbia, OV-102

LAUNCH DATE

12 November 1981

MISSION

- Second shuttle flight of Columbia
- First time a crewed spacecraft is reused in space.
- Testing flight characteristics of the orbiter and launch system.
- Office of Space and Terrestrial Applications-1 payload (OSTA-1).

The mission patch for STS-2 is a simple yet classic design comprising familiar elements used throughout NASA's mission-patch history. The design is dominated by a bald eagle, that traditional emblem of the USA. The US flag forms the eagle's wing while also symbolizing the flight path of the shuttle, which is shown bursting out of the circular patch. The crew names Engle and Truly are shown on the bird's wing, and the name of the shuttle features boldly at the top. The two stars top right represent the two crew members, the second spaceflight for Columbia and the second mission of the programme.

The flight lasted over two days and carried the OSTA-1 (Office of Space and Terrestrial Application-1) scientific-research payload alongside the Remote Manipulator System (RMS) robotic arm, known as Canadarm, which was used to deploy and recapture payloads throughout the Space Shuttle Program. As well as the crew testing the orbiter's flight performance, the on-board OSTA-1 experiments collected scientific data that focused on Earth's atmosphere, oceans and natural resources.

DID YOU KNOW?

Shuttles are also referred to as 'orbiters' or 'orbiter vehicles', hence the designation OV-102 for Columbia. There were five spaceworthy shuttles in total: Columbia, Challenger, Discovery, Atlantis and Endeavour. The first shuttle, Enterprise OV-101, was only designed for atmospheric test flights.

Left to right: Joe Engle, Dick Truly

STS-3

CREW
Jack R. Lousma – Commander
C. Gordon Fullerton – Pilot

SPACECRAFT
Columbia, OV-102

LAUNCH DATE
22 March 1982

MISSION
• Extensive orbital flight characteristic tests of Columbia.
• Office of Space Science-1 scientific payload (OSS-1).

Left to right: Jack Lousma, C. Gordon Fullerton

On the STS-3 patch – created by renowned space artist Robert McCall – we see Columbia with its payload-bay doors wide open and the Remote Manipulator System robotic arm deploying a scientific instrument, most likely the Plasma Diagnostic Package. The bold solar glare behind the shuttle references the thermal test procedures carried out by the crew, in which they exposed the orbiter's top, nose and tail to the Sun for long durations and measured the effects that extreme temperatures had on the vehicle. Protruding from the Sun are three prominent rays that indicate the mission's designation number.

STS-3 was the third spaceflight for Columbia, and included further extensive testing and verification of flight characteristics. The OSS-1 (Office of Space Science-1) payload was used to conduct experiments focused on the orbiter itself, life sciences and space plasma. STS-3 landed at White Sands Space Harbor in New Mexico because of poor weather conditions and flooding at the usual landing site of Edwards Air Force Base, California.

DID YOU KNOW?

STS-3 marked the first time the external fuel tank was not painted white. In an effort to shed more weight (600 pounds/272 kilograms), the UV paint designed to help keep the tank cool was deemed unnecessary, and all future missions flew with its distinctive burnt-orange colour, the natural colour of the insulation coating.

CREW
Thomas K. 'Ken' Mattingly II – Commander
Henry W. 'Hank' Hartsfield Jr – Pilot

SPACECRAFT
Columbia, OV-102

LAUNCH DATE
27 June 1982

MISSION
- Final research and development test flight of the shuttle.
- Department of Defence of Defense payload.

With STS-4 marking the end of the successful research-and-development phase of the Space Shuttle Program, this mission patch shows Columbia triumphantly soaring off into the future and out of the patch itself. Leaving a trail behind her in the colours of the US flag, the number 4 can be seen in the trail, depicting the orbital path of the mission. The shuttle's name is in bold above Earth, while the crew names are at the bottom.

Apollo veteran Ken Mattingly and rookie Henry 'Hank' Hartsfield blasted off from Kennedy Space Center on 27 June 1982, to take Columbia on its final official test flight. The crew would also conduct and deploy a series of scientific experiments, including some supplied by students at Utah State University. Columbia also carried a US Department of Defense classified payload.

DID YOU KNOW?
STS-4 was the last flight to have a crew of just two. After the mission was successfully completed, NASA declared the Space Shuttle fully operational for future space exploration, which saw the shuttle venture into orbit for a period spanning 30 years and a total of 135 missions.

Left to right: Hank Hartsfield, Ken Mattingly

STS-5

CREW

Vance D. Brand – Commander
Robert F. Overmyer – Pilot
Joseph P. Allen – Mission Specialist
William B. Lenoir – Mission Specialist

SPACECRAFT

Columbia, OV-102

LAUNCH DATE

11 November 1982

MISSION

• Deployment of two commercial communications
  satellites, ANIK C-3 and SBS-C.

Left to right: Joseph Allen, Vance Brand, Robert Overmyer,
William Lenoir

For STS-5 we see two commercial communications satellites being deployed from Columbia's payload bay. Both satellites are equipped with their own solid rocket motors, known as the Payload Assist Module (PAM-D), which would place them in an elliptical orbit around Earth. Behind the shuttle is a large blue star with five points, representing the mission number, and around the edge of the insignia are the names of all four crew members, the largest crew of any spacecraft up to this point.

STS-5 was the first mission after being declared fully operational by NASA following four previous test-flight missions. The two commercial communications satellites deployed were ANIK C-3 for TELESAT Canada and SBS-C for Satellite Business Systems. A series of experiments were performed throughout the five-day mission; however, a scheduled spacewalk was cancelled because of a problem with the EVA spacesuit. The mission lasted just over five days, and the crew orbited Earth 82 times.

CREW

Paul J. Weitz – Commander
Karol J. 'Bo' Bobko – Pilot
Donald H. Peterson – Mission Specialist
F. Story Musgrave – Mission Specialist

SPACECRAFT

Challenger, OV-099

LAUNCH DATE

4 April 1983

MISSION

- First flight of Space Shuttle Challenger.
- First shuttle extravehicular activity (EVA).
- Deployment of Tracking and Data Relay Satellite-1 (TDRS-1).

Space Shuttle Challenger made its debut on STS-6, and the mission patch references the maiden flight with the six stars at the top being portrayed as part of the constellation Virgo. They – along with the hexagonal shape of the patch – also give us the designated mission number. As Challenger soars over the Earth, the Tracking and Data Relay Satellite-1 (TDRS-1) can be seen leaving the payload bay and being propelled into orbit by the Inertial Upper Stage booster. The red, white and blue colour scheme references the Stars and Stripes, and around the edge are the astronauts' names and the orbiter name along with the mission designation.

After a series of setbacks during the launch phase caused by hydrogen leaks in the shuttle's main engine and faults with engines two and three, Challenger finally lifted off into space on 4 April 1983. The primary payload was the first Tracking and Data Relay Satellite-1. Astronauts Story Musgrave and Donald Peterson performed the first EVA in the Space Shuttle Program, which lasted over four hours. The mission duration was five days, and 81 orbits were completed.

DID YOU KNOW?

STS-6 was the first shuttle mission to utilize NASA's newly developed lightweight external tank and solid rocket boosters.

Left to right: Donald Peterson, Paul Weitz, F. Story Musgrave, Bo Bobko

CREW

Robert L. 'Bob' Crippen – Commander
Frederick H. 'Rick' Hauck – Pilot
John M. Fabian – Mission Specialist
Sally K. Ride – Mission Specialist
Norman E. Thagard – Mission Specialist

SPACECRAFT

Challenger, OV-099

LAUNCH DATE

18 June 1983

MISSION

• Deployment and recapture of Shuttle Pallet Satellite (SPAS-01).
• Deployment of communications satellites and other scientific experimentation.

Left to right: Sally Ride, John Fabian, Bob Crippen, Norman Thagard, Rick Hauck

The STS-7 mission insignia depicts Challenger orbiting Earth with its Remote Manipulator System arm configured as the number 7 – and there is a further reference to the mission number in the seven white stars. To the right of the patch, sitting underneath the shuttle's wing, is the Sun, containing a graphic that acknowledges the five crew members: four Mars (male) symbols for the four men on board and one Venus (female) symbol for Sally Ride.

During the mission, two communications satellites were deployed, one Canadian and one Indonesian. Also deployed was the Shuttle Pallet Satellite known as SPAS-01. This could carry a vast array of experiments and tests that could be retrieved later by the shuttle's robotic arm and then taken back to Earth for analysis. The crew of STS-7 carried out a series of scientific experiments throughout the mission, including studying the effects of a microgravity environment on an ant colony.

DID YOU KNOW?

Sally K. Ride became the first American woman in space on STS-7. She would fly one more time on board STS-41-G in 1984.

CREW

Richard H. 'Dick' Truly – Commander
Daniel C. Brandenstein – Pilot
Dale A. Gardner – Mission Specialist
Guion S. 'Guy' Bluford Jr – Mission Specialist
William E. 'Bill' Thornton – Mission Specialist

SPACECRAFT

Challenger, OV-099

LAUNCH DATE

30 August 1983

MISSION

- Deployment of the Indian INSAT-1B communications satellite.
- Testing of the Remote Manipulator System under heavy loads.
- Scientific research and experiments.

The STS-8 design is simple yet iconic, showing Challenger rocketing upwards towards space with the orange external tank still attached and the solid rocket boosters in the process of being jettisoned. To the right are eight stars representing the mission number; these are in the form of the constellation Aquila, the eagle, a symbol of the USA. The five astronauts' names encircle the patch, while the orbiter name, Challenger, is in bold letters across the front.

During the six-day mission, the INSAT-1B – a multi-purpose communications-and-weather-observation satellite for the Indian Space Research Organisation – was deployed, and a number of tests were conducted on the Remote Manipulator System to verify the performance of the arm under heavy payloads. As well as the five-man crew, six rats were also on board to allow the study of animal behaviours in microgravity, and a series of other scientific and medical studies were also performed, including further research into the effects of space sickness. STS-8 was the first night launch and landing of the Space Shuttle Program.

DID YOU KNOW?

Guion 'Guy' Bluford became the first African-American astronaut to go into space on STS-8. He flew on four shuttle missions in total between 1983 and 1992, STS-8, STS-61-A, STS-39 and STS-53.

Left to right: Daniel Brandenstein, Dale Gardner, Dick Truly, Bill Thornton, Guy Bluford

CREW

John W. Young – Commander
Brewster H. Shaw – Pilot
Owen K. Garriott – Mission Specialist
Robert A. Parker – Mission Specialist
Ulf D. Merbold – Payload Specialist (ESA)
Byron K. Lichtenberg – Payload Specialist

SPACECRAFT

Columbia, OV-102

LAUNCH DATE

28 November 1983

MISSION

• First mission to carry a Spacelab module into space.

Left to right: Owen Garriott, Byron Lichtenberg, Brewster Shaw, John Young, Ulf Merbold, Robert Parker

The primary payload for STS-9 was Spacelab-1, an orbital science laboratory module built by the European Space Agency (ESA), which remains in the shuttle's payload bay, allowing astronauts to conduct extensive experiments during the mission schedule. Spacelab-1 can be seen sitting inside the open bay of Columbia in this artwork. The main focus of the design shows Columbia leaving a trail behind her illustrating the orbital flight path of the mission and forming the number 9. Nine stars also mark the designated mission number.

STS-9 carried a crew of six astronauts into orbit in November 1983, the largest crew to fly into space on a single spacecraft up to this point. Throughout the ten-day mission, 73 scientific studies were conducted inside the new Spacelab-1 module in the disciplines of astronomy, atmospheric physics, Earth observations, life sciences, materials science, space-plasma physics and technology.

DID YOU KNOW?

German payload specialist Ulf D. Merbold became the first European Space Agency astronaut to travel into space on STS-9. He was also the first non-American to fly on the Space Shuttle.

CREW

Vance D. Brand – Commander
Robert L. 'Hoot' Gibson – Pilot
Bruce McCandless II – Mission Specialist
Ronald E. McNair – Mission Specialist
Robert L. Stewart – Mission Specialist

SPACECRAFT

Challenger, OV-099

LAUNCH DATE

3 February 1984

MISSION

- First untethered EVA using Manned Maneuvering Unit.
- Deployment of WESTAR-VI and PALAPA-B2 satellites.
- First landing of a shuttle at Kennedy Space Center.

The STS-41-B mission patch was designed by artist Robert McCall. Here, Challenger is pictured in the centre with its landing gear deployed. In the right-hand circle is an illustration of an astronaut performing the first untethered EVA, using the Manned Maneuvering Unit (MMU); the left-hand circle shows a satellite being deployed with its Payload Assist Module (PAM-D) engine firing to propel it into orbit.

Bruce McCandless made the first untethered EVA using the MMU jet pack; Robert Stewart also used the MMU and conducted tests for new foot restraints attached to the shuttle's robotic arm. Along with a series of experiments, two communications satellites were deployed, but faulty PAM-D engines prevented them from reaching the desired orbital trajectory.

DID YOU KNOW?

STS-41-B marked a change in mission designations. With NASA's intention to launch many more flights each year, a new system was developed. The first number to follow the letters STS would indicate the US fiscal year in which the flight would take place; the second indicated the launch site (Kennedy Space Center, Florida, was 1 and Vandenberg Air Force Base, California, was 2); and the final letter indicated the launch sequence for that year (A = first launch, B = second, etc.).

Left to right: Robert Stewart, Vance Brand, Ronald McNair, Hoot Gibson, Bruce McCandless

STS-41-C

CREW

Robert L. 'Bob' Crippen – Commander
Francis R. 'Dick' Scobee – Pilot
George D. 'Pinky' Nelson – Mission Specialist
James D. A. 'Ox' van Hoften – Mission Specialist
Terry J. 'TJ' Hart – Mission Specialist

SPACECRAFT

Challenger, OV-099

LAUNCH DATE

6 April 1984

MISSION

• Repair of the Solar Maximum Satellite
• Deployment of the Long Duration Exposure Facility into orbit.

The patch artwork for STS-41-C depicts the objectives of the mission reflected in an astronaut's helmet visor while performing an EVA. With Earth at the top and the Sun's powerful rays spreading across the design, an astronaut can be seen performing repair duties to the faulty Solar Maximum Satellite (SMS) using the Manned Maneuvering Unit jet pack. Above him, Challenger has its payload-bay doors open, and the Long Duration Exposure Facility (LDEF) is deployed via the Remote Manipulator System arm.

The Solar Maximum Satellite had been launched on an unpiloted rocket in 1980, but a failure in its altitude-control system meant that it needed repairs before it could be fully operational. The LDEF, which had been carried into space in Challenger's payload bay, housed 57 scientific experiments designed to study various spacecraft components and the effects on spacecraft systems of exposure to the hostile environment of space for an extended period; after almost six years in orbit, the LDEF was retrieved by shuttle mission STS-32 in 1990.

Left to right: Bob Crippen, TJ Hart, Ox van Hoften, Pinky Nelson, Dick Scobee

DID YOU KNOW?
Experiments conducted during the course of the seven-day STS-41-C mission included a study of honeybees in microgravity provided by the Shuttle Student Involvement Program.

STS-41-D was Discovery's maiden voyage. The mission patch illustrates the shuttle triumphantly flying through space leaving a red, white and blue trail behind it, representing the orbital trajectory of the mission but also leading back to an illustration of an old sailing vessel, marking the transition from the historic sailing ships bearing the name Discovery to the new-era spacecraft of the same name. A large solar array panel called OAST-1 can be seen protruding from the payload bay. The 102-foot (31-metre) solar array consisted of various types of solar cells for testing, which provided valuable data in the development of the International Space Station. There are twelve stars in the artwork, which reference the original mission designation of STS-12.

During the six-day mission, the crew deployed three commercial communications satellites as well as performing a range of different tasks and experiments, including the Continuous Flow Electrophoresis System (CFES) living-cell experiment, a Shuttle Student Involvement Program experiment on the formation of crystals in space, and the Cloud Logic to Optimize Use of Defense Systems experiment (CLOUDS).

DID YOU KNOW?
The crew filmed the mission highlights using a high-definition IMAX camera, which had also been used on the previous mission, STS-41-C.

STS-41-D

CREW

Henry W. 'Hank' Hartsfield Jr – Commander
Michael L. Coats – Pilot
Richard M. 'Mike' Mullane – Mission Specialist
Steven A. Hawley – Mission Specialist
Judith A. Resnik – Mission Specialist
Charles D. Walker – Payload Specialist

SPACECRAFT

Discovery, OV-103

LAUNCH DATE

30 August 1984

MISSION

- First flight of Space Shuttle Discovery.
- Deployment of three commercial communications satellites.
- Testing of the OAST-1 solar array panel.

Left to right: (back) Charles Walker, Judith Resnik; (front) Mike Mullane, Steven Hawley, Hank Hartsfield, Michael Coats

REW

bert L. 'Bob' Crippen – Commander
n A. McBride – Pilot
thryn D. Sullivan – Mission Specialist
lly K. Ride – Mission Specialist
avid C. Leestma – Mission Specialist
arc Garneau – Payload Specialist (CSA)
ul D. Scully-Power – Payload Specialist

PACECRAFT

allenger, OV-099

AUNCH DATE

October 1984

ISSION

Deployment of Earth Radiation Budget Satellite and
conducting experiments from the OSTA-3 payload.
First shuttle mission to carry a crew of seven astronauts
First US woman to perform an EVA.

ft to right: (back) Paul Scully-Power, Bob Crippen,
arc Garneau; (front) Jon McBride, Sally Ride,
thryn Sullivan, David Leestma

An iconic gold astronaut emblem with a plume of smoke around its base to represent the shuttle launch is at the centre of this patch illustrated by artist Patrick Rawlings. Either side of the emblem are clusters of stars; there are seventeen in total as the mission was originally scheduled as STS-17. To the left is the cluster known as the Pleiades, or Seven Sisters, while the stars on the right check the original five crew members: Crippen, McBride, Sullivan, Leestma and Ride. Payload specialists Paul Scully-Power and Marc Garneau from Canada joined the crew at a later date, and the artwork was altered to include their names and a Canadian flag at the bottom of the patch. Beside each astronaut's name is the appropriate male and female symbol. A large billowing Stars and Stripes dominates the upper half of the patch.

The primary payload of STS-41-G was the Earth Radiation Budget Satellite (ERBS), which was deployed shortly after Challenger reached orbit. The shuttle also carried the OSTA-3, which consisted of three experiments: the Shuttle Imaging Radar-B (SIR-B), Measurement of Air Pollution from Satellites (MAPS) and the Feature Identification and Landmark Experiment (FILE). Astronauts Kathryn Sullivan and David Leestma performed an EVA demonstrating the Orbital Refueling System that allows satellites to be refuelled in space.

CREW

Frederick H. 'Rick' Hauck – Commander
David M. Walker – Pilot
Anna L. Fisher – Mission Specialist
Dale A. Gardner – Mission Specialist
Joseph P. Allen – Mission Specialist

SPACECRAFT

Discovery, OV-103

LAUNCH DATE

8 November 1984

MISSION

- Deployment of two communications satellites.
- Retrieval of two faulty satellites already in orbit.

The STS-51-A mission patch – created by artist Stephen R. Hustvedt – sees Discovery soaring through the skies like a bald eagle with the red and white stripes of the American flag in her trail. Earth is present in the background of the design, and two orbital satellites can be seen above to acknowledge the main objectives of the mission. The names of the five crew members appear around the edge of the oval design, which is coloured blue and gold in honour of the US Navy backgrounds of mission commander Rick Hauck and pilot David Walker.

Two communications satellites were deployed into orbit, Canada's ANIK-D2 and the defence-communications satellite LEASAT-1. Another mission objective was the retrieval of two damaged satellites that had been deployed nine months earlier on STS-41-B but failed to reach their correct orbital altitude. With the assistance of the shuttle's robotic arm, Dale Gardner and Joseph Allen conducted EVAs wearing the Manned Maneuvering Unit (MMU) jet packs to capture the two satellites and stow them in Discovery's payload bay.

DID YOU KNOW?

STS-51-A was the final mission to use the MMU jet pack for EVAs. A smaller, more lightweight model named SAFER (Simplified Aid for EVA Rescue) was developed for potential rescue operations, but future EVAs would also rely on the safety of a tether and safety grips.

Left to right: (back) Dale Gardner, David Walker, Anna Fisher, Rick Hauck; (front) Joseph Allen

STS-51-C

CREW

Thomas K. 'Ken' Mattingly II – Commander
Loren J. Shriver – Pilot
Ellison S. Onizuka – Mission Specialist
James F. Buchli – Mission Specialist
Gary E. Payton – Payload Specialist (MSE)

SPACECRAFT

Discovery, OV-103

LAUNCH DATE

24 January 1985

MISSION

• Classified Department of Defense mission.

Left to right: (back) Gary Payton, James Buchli,
Ellison Onizuka; (front) Loren Shriver, Ken Mattingly

STS-51-C was the first shuttle mission completely given over to the US Department of Defense. This is reflected in the mission patch, as the design resembles a slightly modified variation of the emblem for that government department. Five stars across the top of the insignia pay homage to the five crew members, while the shield in the centre features a subtle silhouette of a shuttle blasting off leaving a patriotic trail of red, white and blue in its wake.

The exact details of this mission remain classified; however, NASA reports that a payload belonging to the US Air Force was deployed using the Inertial Upper Stage (IUS) booster, raising the top-secret payload into a higher orbit.

DID YOU KNOW?

Gary Payton was the first astronaut from the Manned Spaceflight Engineer (MSE) programme to venture into space. Operated by the US Air Force, the MSE was formed to train American military personnel as astronauts in order to carry out payload operations on classified shuttle missions reserved for the Department of Defense.

CREW

Karol J. 'Bo' Bobko – Commander
Donald E. Williams – Pilot
M. Rhea Seddon – Mission Specialist
Jeffrey A. Hoffman – Mission Specialist
S. David Griggs – Mission Specialist
Charles D. Walker – Payload Specialist
E. Jake Garn – Payload Specialist

SPACECRAFT

Discovery, OV-103

LAUNCH DATE

12 April 1985

MISSION

- Deployment of two communications satellites.
- Further technological, scientific and medical experiments and tasks.

The mission patch of STS-51-D makes reference to the early days of the USA and how the country has progressed from the days of first colonial pioneers to the technological achievements and advances of modern space exploration. The oval design pictures Earth at the centre with the USA prominent. Space Shuttle Discovery is shown orbiting our planet leaving behind a trail formed of the original US flag, which bore 13 stars in a circle, one for each of the original 13 colonies. Here, like many other mission patches from this period, an extra tab can be seen at the bottom bearing the names of the payload specialists. This was because many of the patches had already been designed by the time the additional crew members were assigned to the mission.

STS-51-D deployed two communications satellites from Discovery's payload bay: the ANIK-C1, which was attached to the Payload Assist Module (PAM-D) to help reach its desired elliptical orbit, and the LEASAT-3. After a series of faults on ignition and despite attempts to repair it, the LEASAT-3 failed to reach its intended orbital trajectory.

Left to right: (back) David Griggs, Charles Walker, Jake Garn; (front) Bo Bobko, Donald Williams, Rhea Seddon, Jeffrey Hoffman

STS-51-B

CREW

Robert F. Overmyer – Commander
Frederick D. Gregory – Pilot
Don L. Lind – Mission Specialist
Norman E. Thagard – Mission Specialist
William E. Thornton – Mission Specialist
Lodewijk van den Berg – Payload Specialist
Taylor G. Wang – Payload Specialist

SPACECRAFT

Challenger, OV-099

LAUNCH DATE

29 April 1985

MISSION

• Spacelab-3 payload.
• Second mission to carry a Spacelab module.

Left to right: (back) Don Lind, Taylor Wang, Norman Thagard, William Thornton, Lodewijk van den Berg; (front) Robert Overmyer, Frederick Gregory

The artwork for the STS-51-B mission patch was produced by Carol Ann Lind, daughter of Don Lind, one of the mission specialists on the flight. Discovery is shown orbiting Earth – represented by the US flag – at the centre of the patch. Surrounding the shuttle are the seven stars of the constellation Pegasus, the winged horse, and Pegasus can be seen ghosted behind the shuttle, flying valiantly through the sky. The seven stars also stand for the seven crew members of the mission.

The primary payload for STS-51-B was the Spacelab-3 science laboratory built by the European Space Agency. Spacelab allowed astronauts to perform a vast array of scientific tasks and experiments in a microgravity environment, including studies in the fields of life sciences, fluid mechanics, atmospheric physics and astronomy. The laboratory also played host to two monkeys and 24 rodents so the effects of weightlessness on animals could be observed.

CREW

Daniel C. Brandenstein – Commander
John O. Creighton – Pilot
Shannon W. Lucid – Mission Specialist
John M. Fabian – Mission Specialist
Steven R. Nagel – Mission Specialist
Patrick Baudry – Payload Specialist (CNES)
Sultan Salman Al-Saud – Payload Specialist (ARABSAT)

SPACECRAFT

Discovery, OV-103

LAUNCH DATE

17 June 1985

MISSION

• Deployment of three communications satellites.
• Scientific research and experiments.

The mission-patch design for STS-51-G pays homage to the advances in American aviation. Discovery is illustrated towards the top with the legendary Wright Flyer directly underneath it. The Wright Brothers famously made the first successful piloted flight of a powered heavier-than-air craft in 1903. That historic flight lasted 12 seconds and was just a few feet off the ground, but, 82 years later, Space Shuttle Discovery would be breaking out of Earth's atmosphere and soaring into space. A bald eagle, the national symbol of the USA, is depicted below, following the same flight path as the two craft above. The astronauts' names surround the patch, while the two payload specialists are on a tag at the bottom along with the national flags of their respective home countries of France (Baudry) and Saudi Arabia (Al-Saud).

The principal objective for STS-51-G was the deployment of three communications satellites: MORELOS-1 (Mexico), ARABSAT-1B (Arab Satellite Communications Organization) and the TELSTAR-3D satellite for AT&T of the USA.

DID YOU KNOW?

Payload specialist Sultan Salman Al-Saud became not only the first Arab and first Muslim to fly into space but also the first member of a royal family to become an astronaut.

Left to right: (back) Shannon Lucid, Steven Nagel, John Fabian, Sultan Salman Al-Saud, Patrick Baudry; (front) Daniel Brandenstein, John Creighton

STS-51-F

STS-51-F

CREW

C. Gordon Fullerton – Commander
Roy D. Bridges Jr – Pilot
F. Story Musgrave – Mission Specialist
Anthony W. England – Mission Specialist
Karl G. Henize – Mission Specialist
Loren W. Acton – Payload Specialist
John-David F. Bartoe – Payload Specialist

SPACECRAFT

Challenger, OV-099

LAUNCH DATE

29 July 1985

MISSION

• Spacelab-2 payload.
• Third mission to carry a Spacelab module.

Left to right: Anthony England, Karl Henize,
Story Musgrave, Gordon Fullerton, Loren Acton,
Roy Bridges, John-David Bartoe

The STS-51-F design, by artist Skip Bradley, shows Challenger exploring the dark void of space with the Sun shining brightly in the distance. The shuttle carried the third Spacelab laboratory into orbit to study a wide range of scientific subjects, including solar physics and stellar astronomy, represented here by the Sun and the stars. The constellation Leo can be seen to the left of the shuttle's tail, and Orion is clearly visible just over the right wing. These star formations are illustrated in the same positions in which they were found during the mission. There are 19 stars in total, marking the fact that this was the 19th flight in the Space Shuttle Program.

This dedicated science mission lasted almost eight days, and the crew performed research and experiments in the fields of life sciences, plasma physics, stellar astronomy, high-energy astrophysics, solar physics, atmospheric physics and technology development. During launch, Challenger's main engine shut down prematurely, which meant the crew had to perform an Abort to Orbit procedure, so placing the shuttle into a lower orbit than intended, but still allowing the mission to continue successfully.

DID YOU KNOW?

Rivals Coca-Cola and Pepsi each developed specially modified cans suitable for use in microgravity. NASA allowed the beverages to be taken on board and tested by the STS-51-F crew, resulting in a PR stunt that was quite literally out of this world.

STS-51-I

CREW

Joe H. Engle – Commander
Richard O. Covey – Pilot
James D. A. 'Ox' van Hoften – Mission Specialist
John M. 'Mike' Lounge – Mission Specialist
William F. Fisher – Mission Specialist

SPACECRAFT

Discovery, OV-103

LAUNCH DATE

27 August 1985

MISSION

• Deployment of three communications satellites and repair of the LEASAT-3 satellite.

The STS-51-I patch design is one that is drenched in American patriotism. As the central focus of the artwork, the American bald eagle is soaring valiantly forward. The eagle's wings leave a trail of red and white stripes behind it, while the background colour is blue, all three colours together being those of the US flag. The white curved line that flows around the eagle's head is symbolic of the shock waves that are formed around the shuttle's nose cone during the re-entry procedure. The 19 stars stand for the intended numerical order of the mission, although STS-51-I became, in fact, the 20th shuttle flight.

The primary payload was three communications satellites. ASC-1 (American Satellite Company) and AUSSAT-1 (Australia) were deployed successfully, but the LEASAT-4 satellite (US military) malfunctioned once it had reached its intended orbit. Astronauts William Fisher and Ox van Hoften performed two EVAs to capture and repair the inoperable LEASAT-3 communications satellite that had been deployed a few months earlier by STS-51-D. After repairing the LEASAT-3, the satellite was activated and successfully redeployed.

Left to right: (back) Ox van Hoften, Mike Lounge, William Fisher; (front) Joe Engle, Richard Covey

STS-51-J

CREW

Karol J. 'Bo' Bobko – Commander
Ronald J. Grabe – Pilot
David C. Hilmers – Mission Specialist
Robert L. Stewart – Mission Specialist
William A. Pailes – Mission Specialist (MSE)

SPACECRAFT

Atlantis, OV-104

LAUNCH DATE

3 October 1985

MISSION

- First flight of Space Shuttle Atlantis.
- Classified Department of Defense mission.

Left to right: (back) David Hilmers, William Pailes;
(front) Robert Stewart, Bo Bobko, Ronald Grabe

This design prominently features the Statue of Liberty, an iconic monument that represents freedom and progress. Mission commander Karol 'Bo' Bobko and pilot Ronald Grabe both hail from New York, so the patch design is a fitting tribute. Space Shuttle Atlantis made its maiden voyage into space on STS-51-J and is pictured ascending boldly above planet Earth.

STS-51-J was the third shuttle mission dedicated to the US Department of Defense and with a classified payload on board. After a four-day mission in space, Atlantis touched down at Edwards Air Force Base in California.

DID YOU KNOW?

During its time in service, Atlantis completed 33 Earth orbital missions for NASA, including STS-135, the final flight of the Space Shuttle Program in 2011. It is now proudly on display at the Kennedy Space Center, Florida.

STS-61-A

CREW

Henry W. 'Hank' Hartsfield Jr – Commander
Steven R. Nagel – Pilot
Bonnie J. Dunbar – Mission Specialist
James F. Buchli – Mission Specialist
Guion S. 'Guy' Bluford Jr – Mission Specialist
Reinhard Furrer – Payload Specialist (DFVLR)
Ernst Messerschmid – Payload Specialist (DFVLR)
Wubbo Ockels – Payload Specialist (ESA)

SPACECRAFT

Challenger, OV-099

LAUNCH DATE

30 October 1985

MISSION

• Spacelab D1 payload operated by West Germany.

The mission-insignia artwork for STS-61-A pays tribute to the joint US/West German collaboration of this landmark mission. The NASA crew names surround the main circle of the patch, while the two German payload specialists are shown at either end of the tab at the bottom; the first Dutch astronaut, Wubbo Ockels, is acknowledged in the centre of the tab with the European Space Agency logo to the right of his name. The design depicts Challenger with its payload bay open exposing the German Spacelab D1 science laboratory. Behind the shuttle is a globe wrapped in the US and German flags. As well as the NASA designation STS-61-A, the mission was known in Germany as D1 (Deutschland 1), shown at the bottom right of the design.

Although shuttle operations on STS-61-A were controlled from Houston, the entire German Spacelab operations were controlled from the German Aerospace Centre in West Germany. The Spacelab D1 laboratory hosted a wealth of experiments, including further studies into the effects of microgravity, life sciences and technology research and development.

DID YOU KNOW?

STS-61-A was the first and only time a shuttle carried a crew of eight astronauts into space.

Left to right: (back) Steven Nagel, Guy Bluford, Ernst Messerschmid, Wubbo Ockels; (front) Reinhard Furrer, Bonnie Dunbar, James Buchli, Hank Hartsfield

STS-61-B

CREW

Brewster H. Shaw Jr – Commander
Bryan D. O'Connor – Pilot
Mary L. Cleave – Mission Specialist
Jerry L. Ross – Mission Specialist
Sherwood C. 'Woody' Spring – Mission Specialist
Rodolfo Neri Vela – Payload Specialist
Charles D. Walker – Payload Specialist

SPACECRAFT

Atlantis, OV-104

LAUNCH DATE

26 November 1985

MISSION

- Deployment of three communications satellites.
- Two structural experiments, ACCESS and EASE.

Left to right: (back) Charles Walker, Jerry Ross, Mary Cleave,
Woody Spring, Rodolfo Neri Vela; (front) Bryan O'Connor,
Brewster Shaw

The mission artwork for Atlantis's second spaceflight portrays the orbiter flying above a bright-blue Earth encircled by a rainbow, a symbol of peace and tranquillity. Space is represented by the stars and stripes of the US flag, while the crew names surround the central design. The two payload specialists for the mission are shown in the bottom tab, and the Mexican flag accompanies astronaut Rodolfo Neri Vela, the first Mexican in space.

Three orbital communications satellites were deployed during the mission, MORELOS-2 (Mexico), AUSSAT-2 (Australia) and SATCOM KU-2 (owned by the RCA Corporation). During the seven-day mission, astronauts Jerry Ross and Woody Spring conducted two separate EVAs, lasting more than 12 hours in total, to erect two structures in space. The ACCESS (Assembly Concept for Construction of Erectable Space Structures) and EASE (Experimental Assembly of Structures in EVA) would test the capability and speed with which astronauts could build large structures in microgravity.

STS-61-C

CREW

Robert L. 'Hoot' Gibson – Commander
Charles F. Bolden Jr – Pilot
Franklin R. Chang-Diaz – Mission Specialist
Steven A. Hawley – Mission Specialist
George D. 'Pinky' Nelson – Mission Specialist
Robert J. Cenker – Payload Specialist
Clarence W. 'Bill' Nelson – Payload Specialist

SPACECRAFT

Columbia, OV-102

LAUNCH DATE

12 January 1986

MISSION

- Deployment of SATCOM KU-1 communications satellite.
- Scientific research.

It is traditional for crew members to design or at least contribute to the concepts behind their mission emblems, and the STS-61-C patch is no different. This bold and bright design features Columbia, the first shuttle into space, pictured at re-entry. The yellow, orange and red pattern that engulfs the shuttle are the shock waves and intense heat the orbiter endures during re-entry into the atmosphere. The lower section of the patch shows the US flag, and the stars in the upper section are the constellation Draco.

The primary payload for this mission was the SATCOM KU-1, an RCA Corporation communications satellite that used a more powerful Payload Assist Module (PAM-D2) to boost it into the desired orbit. The crew also carried out a range of scientific experiments and studies in the fields of stellar astronomy, seed germination, chemical reactions, egg hatching, blood storage, atmospheric physics and the effects of microgravity environments among others. The crew intended to observe and photograph Halley's Comet for an experiment named CHAMP (Comet Halley Active Monitoring Program), but the camera failed to work.

Left to right: Robert Cenker, Charles Bolden, Bill Nelson, Steven Hawley, Pinky Nelson, Hoot Gibson, Franklin Chang-Diaz

STS-51-L

CREW

Francis R. 'Dick' Scobee – Commander
Michael J. Smith – Pilot
Ellison S. Onizuka – Mission Specialist
Judith A. Resnik – Mission Specialist
Ronald E. McNair – Mission Specialist
S. Christa McAuliffe – Payload Specialist
Gregory B. Jarvis – Payload Specialist

SPACECRAFT

Challenger, OV-099

LAUNCH DATE

28 January 1986

MISSION

- Intended deployment of Tracking and Data Relay Satellite-2.
- Catastrophic failure 73 seconds into the launch procedure resulting in the loss of the shuttle and claiming the lives of all seven crew members.

Left to right: (back) Ellison Onizuka, Christa McAuliffe, Gregory Jarvis, Judith Resnik; (front) Michael Smith, Dick Scobee, Ronald McNair

The STS-51-L mission insignia features Challenger leaving the launch site in Florida and soaring into space for what would have been its tenth flight. One of the mission objectives was to observe and photograph Halley's Comet, which is illustrated at the top of the design with the US flag in the background. The mission achieved worldwide interest and publicity because Christa McAuliffe, a schoolteacher from New Hampshire, would be part of the crew and be the first civilian in space. In an effort to generate student interest in space exploration, NASA had initiated a Teacher in Space Project. The crew are represented by seven stars in the flag, and their names encircle the main artwork with the payload specialists in the tab. A bright-red apple is shown next to McAuliffe's name, a symbol long associated with teachers, when apples and other fruit were given by parents to pay for their children's education.

Just 73 seconds into the launch sequence, disaster struck as the shuttle exploded, resulting in the loss of the entire crew. Flight operations were put on hold in order to determine the cause of the tragedy, and the next shuttle mission would not be launched for almost three years.

DID YOU KNOW?

The Challenger explosion came about through a faulty O-ring in the right-side solid rocket booster; a flame caused the booster to detach itself and rupture the external fuel tank.

STS-26 is NASA's 'return-to-flight' mission after the tragic loss of Challenger and its crew on STS-51-L. This bold design, by artist Stephen R. Hustvedt, expresses new beginnings with the Sun rising over the horizon, ushering in a new dawn of Space Shuttle exploration. The shuttle can be seen reaching high into space, leaving a plume of smoke in its trail after a safe and successful launch. The red 'wing' icon that intersects the trail is that used in NASA's logo and pays homage to the space agency. The seven stars are included as a tribute to the seven crew members who lost their lives on Challenger and form the shape of the Big Dipper asterism, a cluster of stars that is easily visible on any clear night.

Nearly three years after the Challenger disaster, the five astronauts of STS-26 arrived in orbit to embark on a four-day mission. The primary payload was the Tracking and Data Relay Satellite-3 (TDRS-3). The satellite was deployed successfully and placed into a geosynchronous orbit. The crew continued with in-flight duties as well as conducting a series of experiments throughout the mission duration. These included an experiment on the aggregation of red blood cells under microgravity, protein crystal growth and two Shuttle Student Involvement Program experiments.

DID YOU KNOW?

STS-26 was the 26th mission of the Space Shuttle Program. From this point on, NASA reverted to the original numbering system.

CREW

Frederick H. 'Rick' Hauck – Commander
Richard O. Covey – Pilot
John M. 'Mike' Lounge – Mission Specialist
George D. 'Pinky' Nelson – Mission Specialist
David C. Hilmers – Mission Specialist

SPACECRAFT

Discovery, OV-103

LAUNCH DATE

29 September 1988

MISSION

- 'Return-to-flight' mission.
- Deployment of Tracking and Data Relay Satellite-3.

Left to right: David Hilmers, Richard Covey, Pinky Nelson, Rick Hauck, Mike Lounge

CREW

Robert L. 'Hoot' Gibson – Commander
Guy S. Gardner – Pilot
Richard M. 'Mike' Mullane – Mission Specialist
Jerry L. Ross – Mission Specialist
William M. Shepherd – Mission Specialist

SPACECRAFT

Atlantis, OV-104

LAUNCH DATE

2 December 1988

MISSION

Classified Department of Defense mission.

Left to right: Guy Gardner, William Shepherd, Hoot Gibson, Mike Mullane, Jerry Ross

More than three years since Atlantis last flew, this vibrant STS-27 mission patch features the shuttle triumphantly launching into space once again. The rainbow behind the craft is all about optimism for a new beginning for the programme following the loss of Challenger in January 1986. The gallant Challenger crew are once again honoured, this time by the seven bold yellow stars scattered throughout the design.

STS-27 was a four-day classified mission dedicated to the US Department of Defense. It was the third flight for Atlantis, the third full Department of Defense mission and the third spaceflight for mission commander Robert L. Gibson.

DID YOU KNOW?
During lift-off, the STS-27 shuttle suffered damage to the heat shield (thermal-protection system) of its right wing. NASA decided the shuttle was safe for re-entry, and Atlantis touched down safely at Edwards Air Force Base in California. The extent of further damage inflicted by the intense heat of re-entry was so severe, however, that the crew were very fortunate the shuttle remained intact.

CREW

Michael L. Coats – Commander
John E. Blaha – Pilot
James P. Bagian – Mission Specialist
James F. Buchli – Mission Specialist
Robert C. Springer – Mission Specialist

SPACECRAFT

Discovery, OV-103

LAUNCH DATE

13 March 1989

MISSION

• Deployment of Tracking and Data Relay Satellite-4.

The artwork for the STS-29 patch features Discovery boldly flying towards the viewer with a stylized depiction of the engines firing behind her. This simple yet dynamic design captures the spirit of NASA's determination to press forward with space exploration and look towards the future. The ribbon-style border gives the insignia a more modern three-dimensional feel, and the red, white and blue colour scheme recalls the Stars and Stripes. The Challenger crew are again acknowledged in the seven stars in the red border. The patch artwork was created by graphic artist David Russell.

During the five-day mission, Discovery deployed the Tracking and Data Relay Satellite-4 (TDRS-4) into a geosynchronous orbit. The crew performed a range of tasks, including experiments to examine the effects of bone healing in rats while in a microgravity environment, an experiment with chromosomes and plant cell division and a protein crystal growth experiment. The crew used a high-definition IMAX camera to film the Earth from space.

Left to right: James Bagian, John Blaha, Robert Springer, Michael Coats, James Buchli

STS-30

CREW

David M. Walker – Commander
Ronald J. Grabe – Pilot
Norman E. Thagard – Mission Specialist
Mary L. Cleave – Mission Specialist
Mark C. Lee – Mission Specialist

SPACECRAFT

Atlantis, OV-104

LAUNCH DATE

4 May 1989

MISSION

• Deployed the Magellan probe on a trajectory to explore Venus.

Left to right: Ronald Grabe, David Walker, Norman Thagard, Mary Cleave, Mark Lee

The crew members of STS-30 designed this insignia alongside graphic artist Sean Collins to illustrate the interplanetary nature of the mission. This was the first time an unpiloted spacecraft to another planet would be deployed from a shuttle. The Magellan probe was launched from the shuttle's payload bay and put on a trajectory towards Venus, a journey that would take 15 months. The probe's objective was to orbit Venus and survey the planet's terrain, relaying data back to mission control. The design depicts the Sun and the first three planets of our solar system: Mercury, Venus and Earth. The red ring around Earth represents the orbit trajectory of Atlantis, while the red curve moving towards and encircling Venus plots that of the Magellan probe's journey. The sailing ship is of the kind that Portuguese explorer Ferdinand Magellan commanded during the 16th-century Spanish expeditions that resulted in the first circumnavigation of our world. Like those of the previous three shuttle missions, this patch also features seven stars to remember the Challenger crew. The cluster of five stars on the left also honours the five astronauts of STS-30.

As well as the successful deployment of the Magellan probe, the crew of this four-day mission also carried out a number of scientific research duties and experiments in the microgravity environment.

CREW

Brewster H. Shaw Jr – Commander
Richard N. Richards – Pilot
James C. Adamson – Mission Specialist
David C. Leestma – Mission Specialist
Mark N. Brown – Mission Specialist

SPACECRAFT

Columbia, OV-102

LAUNCH DATE

8 August 1989

MISSION

• Classified Department of Defense mission.

Patriotism is at the heart of this artwork for the STS-28 patch, created by artist Sean Collins and the crew. As Columbia enters Earth's atmosphere, an American bald eagle – iconic emblem of the USA that features on the country's Great Seal – guides her down for a safe landing. The shuttle and eagle descend towards Earth leaving contrails of red and white stripes behind them on a blue background, symbolizing the American flag. Columbia touched down at Edwards Air Force Base in California, which is located at the very bottom edge of the patch: you can see southern California, with Baja California in Mexico just above it.

STS-28 was the fourth shuttle flight dedicated to the US Department of Defense and carrying a classified payload on board.

DID YOU KNOW?
The five-day mission of STS-28 was Columbia's first spaceflight for three and a half years.

Left to right: Richard Richards, Mark Brown, Brewster Shaw, James Adamson, David Leestma

CREW

Donald E. Williams – Commander
Michael J. McCulley – Pilot
Franklin R. Chang-Díaz – Mission Specialist
Shannon W. Lucid – Mission Specialist
Ellen S. Baker – Mission Specialist

SPACECRAFT

Atlantis, OV-104

LAUNCH DATE

8 October 1989

MISSION

• Deployment of the unpiloted Galileo spacecraft to orbit Jupiter.

Left to right: Shannon Lucid, Donald Williams,
Franklin Chang-Díaz, Michael McCulley, Ellen Baker

Central to the STS-34 mission patch is a beautiful top-view illustration of Atlantis with the unpiloted Galileo spacecraft above the shuttle's payload-bay doors. Galileo was deployed and sent on a six-year voyage to Jupiter, the fifth and largest planet in our solar system. It became the first spacecraft to orbit the gas giant, which is shown behind the shuttle's right wing. At the bottom of the artwork the Sun rises over Earth to symbolize how human exploration of the solar system will contribute to a better understanding of our own planet. Once again, the seven stars in the design are a tribute to the crew that perished on Challenger.

The Galileo spacecraft entered Jupiter's orbit in December 1995. The original plans were for it to orbit and survey the planet for two years, but NASA extended the mission, and Galileo continued to relay scientific data back to Earth until 2003 when the programme was terminated. After Atlantis had successfully deployed Galileo, the crew began to perform other in-flight tasks including an experiment with growth hormone crystal distribution, a Shuttle Student Involvement Program experiment and photographing Earth with a high-definition IMAX camera.

DID YOU KNOW?
STS-34 was named after Galileo Galilei, the Italian astronomer and physicist who discovered four of Jupiter's largest moons in the early 17th century.

CREW

Frederick D. Gregory – Commander
John E. Blaha – Pilot
F. Story Musgrave – Mission Specialist
Manley L. 'Sonny' Carter Jr – Mission Specialist
Kathryn C. Thornton – Mission Specialist

SPACECRAFT

Discovery, OV-103

LAUNCH DATE

22 November 1989

MISSION

• Classified Department of Defense mission.

STS-33 is often referred to as the 'Falcon Flight' by mission control, and the design depicts a stylized falcon soaring from left to right. The falcon was chosen by the crew to represent their mission because it stands for courage, intelligence, tenacity and a love of flight. With its extraordinary vision and the ability to fly at incredible speeds, the falcon can be seen looking far beyond the boundaries of the patch, seeking out new horizons in the outer reaches of space to show humankind's courage and determination in extending our knowledge of the universe and our continued commitment to space exploration. The boldly extended red wings are the stripes of the US flag, showing America's desire to expand its understanding of the solar system and beyond. Earth is in the background surrounded by a yellow ring, showing the orbit trajectory of the mission. The gold star on the right-hand side honours astronaut S. David Griggs, who was due to be the pilot on this mission but was tragically killed in June 1989 when the vintage World War II AT-6 Texan he was flying crashed.

STS-33 was the fifth shuttle mission dedicated entirely to the US Department of Defense. Discovery carried a classified payload on a five-day mission, after which it touched down at Edwards Air Force Base, California, on 27 November 1989.

Left to right: Kathryn Thornton, Sonny Carter, Frederick Gregory, John Blaha, Story Musgrave

STS-32

CREW

Daniel C. Brandenstein – Commander
James D. Wetherbee – Pilot
Bonnie J. Dunbar – Mission Specialist
G. David Low – Mission Specialist
Marsha S. Ivins – Mission Specialist

SPACECRAFT

Columbia, OV-102

LAUNCH DATE

9 January 1990

MISSION

• Deployment of LEASAT-5 communications satellite.
• Rendezvous and retrieval of the LDEF scientific module.

Left to right: Marsha Ivins, Daniel Brandenstein, David Low,
James Wetherbee, Bonnie Dunbar

Here we find Columbia in space with its payload-bay doors wide open and the Remote Manipulator System robotic arm extended. The large module floating over Earth is the Long Duration Exposure Facility (LDEF), which was retrieved using the robotic arm. The LEASAT-5 communications satellite is on the right of the patch with its booster firing, propelling the satellite into a geosynchronous orbit. A series of scientific and medical experiments was undertaken in preparation for the Extended Duration Orbiter (EDO) missions that began two years later with STS-50. The caduceus on the left side of the circular border represents the medical experiments and the crystal on the right states the materials-science nature of the mission. Earth is illustrated at the bottom with the Sun rising over its horizon. There are five stars, one each for every crew member. Three of the stars are positioned to the left of the shuttle and two to the right, which makes 3-2, or the number 32. The Sun shoots out seven orange rays, which are in memoriam of the seven crew members who died on STS-51-L.

After successful deployment of the LEASAT-5 satellite, Columbia made her rendezvous with the LDEF module, which had been launched into space by STS-41-C. After almost six years accumulating data about the effects on spacecraft components of long durations in space, the shuttle's robotic arm captured it and placed it in the payload bay. The data collected from the LDEF proved invaluable in the development of the International Space Station.

STS-36

John O. Creighton – Commander
John H. Casper – Pilot
Pierre J. Thuot – Mission Specialist
David C. Hilmers – Mission Specialist
Richard M. 'Mike' Mullane – Mission Specialist

SPACECRAFT

Atlantis, OV-104

LAUNCH DATE

28 February 1990

MISSION

• Classified Department of Defense mission.

STS-36 was a highly classified mission for the US Department of Defense, and the patch focuses, as with previous classified shuttle missions, on a theme of national pride and patriotism. The dominant feature is once again a proud American bald eagle backdropped by a vibrant US flag merging into a starry night sky. The night launch occurred at 2.50 a.m. (EST), and the artwork captures this beautifully. The eagle was once again chosen to express the strength and determination of America and its desire to look beyond the boundaries of our Earth, extending human knowledge and venturing further into the unknown reaches of space. The flag is there to convey the patriotism and love of country that each crew member possessed and signifies the honour bestowed upon them for undertaking this mission of national defence. The shuttle can be seen blasting towards space at the centre of the design, a reminder to all of the essential role space exploration plays in the security and freedom of the USA. Graphic artist David Russell created the final artwork for this iconic patch with creative direction from the crew of Atlantis.

Atlantis carried a classified payload for its sixth voyage. The mission lasted four days and ten hours and was also the sixth shuttle flight dedicated to the Department of Defense. After travelling a total distance of 1.9 million miles (3 million kilometres), Atlantis re-entered Earth's atmosphere, bringing the top-secret mission to a close. Touchdown was at Edwards Air Force Base, California, on 4 March 1990.

Left to right: Pierre Thuot, John Casper, John Creighton, Mike Mullane, David Hilmers

STS-31

CREW

Loren J. Shriver – Commander
Charles F. Bolden Jr – Pilot
Steven A. Hawley – Mission Specialist
Bruce McCandless II – Mission Specialist
Kathryn D. Sullivan – Mission Specialist

SPACECRAFT

Discovery, OV-103

LAUNCH DATE

24 April 1990

MISSION

• Deployment of the Hubble Space Telescope.

Left to right: Charles Bolden, Steven Hawley, Loren Shriver,
Bruce McCandless, Kathryn Sullivan

The subject on this mission patch is the deployment of the Hubble Space Telescope from Discovery's payload bay, shown against a stylized cosmic backdrop. Named after the American astronomer Edwin Hubble, the purpose of the telescope is to collect images and light sources from planets, galaxies, nebulae and other celestial objects and so gain a better understanding of the universe. Hubble's Law is a theory to determine the distances of these faraway galaxies and their velocities. In astronomy, the terms 'redshift' and 'blueshift' refer to how light shifts to the red end of the visible spectrum the further away an object moves in space, whereas it shifts towards the blue end the closer it moves to the viewer. The red-and-blue trajectory on the mission patch pays tribute to Hubble's work and the colour shifts that were vital to his discoveries as well as symbolizing the new phenomena that the Hubble Space Telescope will reveal.

STS-31 lasted five days and, in addition to conducting the deployment of Hubble, the crew performed a range of other in-flight experiments and tasks including using the IMAX Cargo Bay Camera to document operations outside the cabin.

DID YOU KNOW?

In 1929, Edwin Hubble discovered the presence of other galaxies and concluded that the universe was expanding and that galaxies were moving further away from each other.

CREW

Richard N. Richards – Commander
Robert D. Cabana – Pilot
William M. Shepherd – Mission Specialist
Bruce E. Melnick – Mission Specialist
Thomas D. Akers – Mission Specialist

SPACECRAFT

Discovery, OV-103

LAUNCH DATE

6 October 1990

MISSION

• Deployment of the Ulysses solar exploration spacecraft

The STS-41 crew designed this insignia with the assistance of graphic artist David Russell to portray the objective of their mission: the deployment of the unpiloted Ulysses solar-exploration spacecraft. Ulysses was a joint European Space Agency–NASA probe, which was sent to study the uncharted north and south poles of the Sun. The red three-pronged trajectory that can be seen exiting the shuttle's payload bay references the design of the iconic badge that every astronaut receives upon completing their training and is also a tribute to the astronauts who have lost their lives in the pursuit of space exploration. After merging into one red trajectory it proceeds on a course to swing around Jupiter, providing Ulysses with a gravitational direction change that will place it in a polar orbit around our star. The orbit is marked by the red trajectory shooting up over the blazing Sun with the silver teardrop representing Ulysses and the incredible speeds (in excess of 100,000 m.p.h./160,000 k.p.h.) it attained. Discovery can be seen over Florida and the southeastern US coast. The five crew members all have stars around the edge of the patch, four gold and one silver.

The Ulysses probe was deployed successfully six hours into the mission. The crew conducted many other tasks during the four-day flight, including the Shuttle Solar Backscatter Ultraviolet experiment, the Chromosome and Plant Cell Division experiment, Investigations into Polymer Membrane Processing and a Shuttle Student Involvement Program experiment.

Left to right: (back) Bruce Melnick, Thomas Akers, William Shepherd; (front) Robert Cabana, Richard Richards

CREW

Richard O. Covey – Commander
Frank L. Culbertson Jr – Pilot
Robert C. Springer – Mission Specialist
Carl J. Meade – Mission Specialist
Charles D. Gemar – Mission Specialist

SPACECRAFT

Atlantis, OV-104

LAUNCH DATE

15 November 1990

MISSION

Classified Department of Defense mission.

Left to right: Charles Gemar, Frank Culberston, Robert Springer, Richard Covey, Carl Meade

The STS-38 patch was conceived with a desire to focus on the efforts of the entire Space Shuttle Program. The top section features Atlantis embarking on its fourth classified mission for the US Department of Defense. The stylized yellow-and-orange burn of the shuttle's Orbital Maneuvering System engines thrusts the shuttle forward, suggesting NASA's ongoing determination and commitment to space exploration. The bottom half of the patch is a desaturated mirror image of the top, designed to honour the thousands of men and women working behind the scenes who each make a vital contribution to the success of the programme.

While sitting on the launch pad in June and July 1990, a hydrogen fuel leak in the orbiter's external tank meant that Atlantis had to be rolled back to the Vehicle Assembly Building (VAB) for repairs. After all the repair work was completed, Atlantis arrived back on the pad on 12 October and launched a month later on 15 November.

DID YOU KNOW?

While parked outside the VAB awaiting repairs, STS-38 was caught in a hail storm and suffered damage to its heat-shield tiles, requiring further maintenance work.

CREW

Vance D. Brand – Commander
Guy S. Gardner – Pilot
Jeffrey A. Hoffman – Mission Specialist
John M. 'Mike' Lounge – Mission Specialist
Robert A. Parker – Mission Specialist
Samuel T. Durrance – Payload Specialist
Ronald A. Parise – Payload Specialist

SPACECRAFT

Columbia, OV-102

LAUNCH DATE

2 December 1990

MISSION

• ASTRO-1, consisting of four ultraviolet telescopes and one X-ray telescope.

The insignia artwork for STS-35 was developed by the crew and was designed to highlight that the focus of this mission was astronomical research. Columbia carried the ASTRO-1 observatory inside its payload bay. ASTRO-1 consisted of four powerful telescopes: the Hopkins Ultraviolet Telescope, the Wisconsin Ultraviolet Photo-Polarimeter Experiment, the Ultraviolet Imaging Telescope and the Broad Band X-Ray Telescope. The design features a silhouetted shuttle soaring above Earth leaving a trajectory trail of the red and white stripes of the US flag. Orion, one of the most recognized constellations in the night sky, can be seen to the left of the shuttle as a symbol of astronomy. The overall colour scheme once again suggests the Stars and Stripes and thus the national pride Americans felt for the Space Shuttle Program.

Following a series of setbacks involving hydrogen fuel leaks, Columbia's original launch date of 16 May was pulled. The next launch, on 30 May, was also cancelled and the orbiter rolled back to the Vehicle Assembly Building. On 9 August, Columbia was transferred back to launch pad 39A for a number of intended launch dates, but, once again, a series of fuel leaks and payload malfunctions meant the mission had to be put on hold. Columbia was moved off pad 39A to allow STS-38 to continue with its mission, but STS-35 eventually got the all-clear to launch on 2 December 1990.

Left to right: (back) Robert Parker, Ronald Parise, Jeffrey Hoffman, Samuel Durrance; (front) Guy Gardner, Vance Brand, Mike Lounge

CREW

Steven R. Nagel – Commander
Kenneth D. Cameron – Pilot
Jerry L. Ross – Mission Specialist
Jerome 'Jay' Apt – Mission Specialist
Linda M. Godwin – Mission Specialist

SPACECRAFT

Atlantis, OV-104

LAUNCH DATE

5 April 1991

MISSION

• Deployment of the Compton Gamma Ray Observatory.

Left to right: Kenneth Cameron, Jay Apt, Steven Nagel,
Jerry Ross, Linda Godwin

This eye-catching mission patch shows the deployment of the Compton Gamma Ray Observatory (CGRO) by STS-37. The CGRO was an astrophysical satellite designed to detect high-energy radiation called gamma rays. Within the bold red border of the mission patch, Atlantis is illustrated alongside the CGRO. The two spacecraft are joined by a representation of the Greek letter gamma in a colour scheme that suggests the presence of electromagnetic radiation. The connecting symbol also reiterates the importance of the relationship between human spaceflight and unpiloted space exploration in order to achieve a greater understanding of the universe. The southeast corner of the USA, along with the Florida launch site for the shuttle programme, is visible in dark blue at the bottom. There are three stars at the top of the mission patch and a cluster of seven on the left, making 3-7, the mission number 37.

The CGRO satellite was deployed three days into the mission. The high-gain antenna of the CGRO failed to release, and an unscheduled spacewalk by Jerry Ross and Jay Apt was required to fix the fault. Two more scheduled spacewalks were performed by Ross and Apt during the six days in orbit.

CREW

Michael L. Coats – Commander
L. Blaine Hammond Jr – Pilot
Guion S. 'Guy' Bluford Jr – Mission Specialist
Gregory J. Harbaugh – Mission Specialist
Richard J. Hieb – Mission Specialist
Donald R. McMonagle – Mission Specialist
Charles L. Veach – Mission Specialist

SPACECRAFT

Discovery, OV-103

LAUNCH DATE

28 April 1991

MISSION

• Unclassified Department of Defense mission.

The seven-man crew of STS-39 wanted their insignia to highlight the objectives of this unclassified US Department of Defense mission. The skywards-pointing arrowhead shape of the patch states the mission's aim of gathering knowledge about Earth's atmosphere and the environment of the universe. The cluster of yellow stars is in the form of Aquila, the Eagle, so suggesting the iconic bald eagle of the USA. The brightest star in the constellation, Altair, projects a radiant spectrum over Earth in the colours of the Stars and Stripes as well as suggesting those of the ultraviolet, X-ray, visible and infrared electromagnetic radiation that will be studied by the scientific payloads on board the shuttle.

STS-39 was the first dedicated Department of Defense mission that was largely unclassified. The military payloads on board were the Air Force Program-675 (AFP-675), the Infrared Background Signature Survey (IBSS) with Critical Ionization Velocity (CIV), the Chemical Release Observation (CRO), the Shuttle Pallet Satellite-II (SPAS-II) and the Space Test Payload-1 (STP-1). Discovery carried just one classified payload on this mission

Left to right: Charles Veach, Donald McMonagle, Gregory Harbaugh, Michael Coats, Blaine Hammond, Richard Hieb, Guy Bluford

91

STS-40

CREW

Bryan D. O'Connor – Commander
Sidney M. Gutierrez – Pilot
James P. Bagian – Mission Specialist
Tamara E. Jernigan – Mission Specialist
M. Rhea Seddon – Mission Specialist
F. Drew Gaffney – Payload Specialist
Millie Hughes-Fulford – Payload Specialist

SPACECRAFT

Columbia, OV-102

LAUNCH DATE

5 June 1991

MISSION

• Spacelab Life Sciences-1 mission (SLS-1).

Left to right: Drew Gaffney, Bryan O'Connor, Millie Hughes-Fulford, Tamara Jernigan, Rhea Seddon, Sidney Gutierrez, James Bagian

STS-40 was the fifth mission to carry a Spacelab science laboratory into orbit and the first to be dedicated entirely to life sciences. 'Spacelab Life Sciences-1 (SLS-1)' is visible on the patch above a black-and-white night view of Earth, with the USA clearly in view. A Native American symbol for the Sun spreads a colourful band, symbolizing the early history of the land that became the USA and way that nation continues to push at the frontiers of space exploration. The seven stars in the blue sky represent the crew members of this mission. The centre of the patch shows the shuttle leaving a trail in a double helix, the molecular shape of the double-stranded DNA molecule found in every living being, a nod to the life-sciences nature of the mission and the human contribution to exploring the universe.

At the top we see an adaptation of Leonardo da Vinci's *The Vitruvian Man*, with its idealized depiction of the proportions of the human body. The figure has one foot touching Earth, while its arms reach into the shuttle's trajectory to symbolize humankind's desire and determination to leave Earth and extend our knowledge of the universe. The artwork was produced by artist Sean Collins with creative guidance by the crew. If you look closely on the stomach of *The Vitruvian Man* you can see the artist's name.

DID YOU KNOW?
Life-science experiments on SLS-1 were conducted using 30 rodents and thousands of tiny jellyfish.

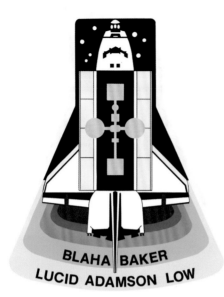

BLAHA BAKER
LUCID ADAMSON LOW

STS-43

CREW

John E. Blaha – Commander
Michael A. Baker – Pilot
Shannon W. Lucid – Mission Specialist
James C. Adamson – Mission Specialist
G. David Low – Mission Specialist

SPACECRAFT

Atlantis, OV-104

LAUNCH DATE

2 August 1991

MISSION

• Deployment of Tracking and Data Relay Satellite-5.

The STS-43 mission patch replicates the iconic shape of a Mercury capsule, America's first manned spacecraft. In honour of Alan Shepard's historic suborbital flight on board Freedom 7 in 1961, the STS-43 insignia celebrates thirty years of American space exploration, from Project Mercury to the Space Transportation System. The light-blue-to-black banding shows the orbiter's skywards journey from Earth into space. The crew's primary payload was the Tracking and Data Relay Satellite-5 (TDRS-5), a device to improve communication with future NASA space missions and provide superior relay of data. The TDRS-5 is shown in gold leaving the shuttle's payload bay. There are four stars at the top left of the patch and three stars top right, indicating the mission designation: 43.

The TDRS-5 became the fourth TDRS to be sent into orbit – TDRS-2 had been destroyed five years earlier in the Challenger explosion. Six hours into the STS-43 mission, the TDRS-5 was propelled into a geosynchronous Earth orbit. The crew carried out a vast array of medical and materials-science experiments to prepare for future long-duration flights.

Left to right: Shannon Lucid, James Adamson, John Blaha, David Low, Michael Baker

CREW

John O. Creighton – Commander

Kenneth S. Reightler Jr – Pilot

James F. Buchli – Mission Specialist

Charles D. Gemar – Mission Specialist

Mark N. Brown – Mission Specialist

SPACECRAFT

Discovery, OV-103

LAUNCH DATE

12 September 1991

MISSION

• Deployment of Upper Atmosphere Research Satellite.

Left to right: Mark Brown, Charles Gemar, John Creighton, James Buchli, Kenneth Reightler

The primary mission objective for STS-48 was the deployment of the Upper Atmospheric Research Satellite (UARS). The satellite conducted extensive studies of Earth's atmosphere, specifically the troposphere, which is where almost all Earth's weather takes place. As Discovery soars across the front of the patch, the trajectory of the UARS is shown in yellow as it leaves the shuttle to begin orbiting Earth. The satellite is named in the bold letters UARS at the top. The small triangular device above UARS suggests the satellite's solar panel. The background illustrates a cloudy Earth with a colourful band showing the layers of the atmosphere. The colours shoot up towards the UARS in acknowledgement of the valuable data being gathered by the satellite. The UARS would begin analysing the atmosphere during autumn, which is when the stars featured in the artwork are visible in the northern hemisphere. The triangular shape of the mission patch itself represents the relationship between the three atmospheric processes that determine Earth's atmosphere, structure and behaviour: chemistry, dynamics and energy. The crew of Discovery designed this mission patch with graphic artist Sean Collins.

The crew performed a number of experiments and deployed several other satellites from Discovery's payload bay. The mission lasted over five days and completed 81 revolutions of Earth before landing at Edwards Air Force Base, California, on 18 September 1991.

STS-44

CREW

Frederick D. Gregory – Commander
Terence T. 'Tom' Henricks – Pilot
F. Story Musgrave – Mission Specialist
Mario Runco Jr – Mission Specialist
James S. Voss – Mission Specialist
Thomas J. Hennen – Payload Specialist

SPACECRAFT

Atlantis, OV-104

LAUNCH DATE

24 November 1991

MISSION

- Unclassified Department of Defense mission.
- Deployment of Defense Support Program satellite.

Designed by the crew of Atlantis with artist Sean Collins, the STS-44 mission patch illustrates the nature of this unclassified mission for the US Department of Defense. While orbiting Earth, the crew would deploy the Defense Support Program satellite, designed to detect the launch of missiles, spacecraft and nuclear detonations as part of America's early-warning system. The centre of the patch sees Atlantis blasting off towards space, and its trajectory is in the form of the US flag to show America's commitment to protecting itself and its allies. The stars in the flag underline the USA's position at the forefront of space exploration and its continued quest for knowledge about the solar system and beyond. The six large stars shown in the blackness of space are the gallant crew members on this important mission, while the smaller stars in the background honour the unsung heroes who work tirelessly behind the scenes.

The Defense Support Program satellite was successfully deployed on the first day. This dedicated Department of Defense mission also carried out a number of tasks and experiments including the Extended Duration Orbiter Medical Project, a series of studies and experiments in support of Extended Duration Orbiter missions that began in 1992.

Left to right: Tom Henricks, James Voss, Frederick Gregory, Thomas Hennen, Story Musgrave, Mario Runco

STS-42

CREW

Ronald J. Grabe – Commander
Stephen S. Oswald – Pilot
Norman E. Thagard – Mission Specialist
David C. Hilmers – Mission Specialist
William F. Readdy – Mission Specialist
Roberta L. Bondar – Payload Specialist (CSA)
Ulf D. Merbold – Payload Specialist (ESA)

SPACECRAFT

Discovery, OV-103

LAUNCH DATE

22 January 1992

MISSION

• Spacelab mission.
• International Microgravity Laboratory-1.

Left to right: Stephen Oswald, Roberta Bondar,
Norman Thagard, Ronald Grabe, David Hilmers,
Ulf Merbold, William Readdy

The STS-42 patch features Discovery oriented in a quiescent, tail-to-Earth gravity-gradient attitude to support the microgravity experiments on which the mission focused. The shuttle's payload-bay doors are wide open, exposing the International Microgravity Laboratory-1 (IML-1). Using a pressurized Spacelab module, the IML-1 was used to conduct research on the human nervous system in microgravity and to study the effects of microgravity on other life forms, including shrimp eggs, fruit fly eggs and bacteria. There are four large stars to the left of the insignia and two above the shuttle, giving us 42, the designated number of the mission. The crew of this research flight are featured around the border. The Canadian nationality of Roberta Bondar is represented by a red maple leaf, and Ulf Merbold from Germany has the European Space Agency insignia next to his name. The single gold star shining above Earth is in honour of astronaut Manley L. 'Sonny' Carter Jr, who was tragically killed in a commuter airline crash. Carter had previously flown on STS-33 and was originally assigned as a mission specialist aboard STS-42 before the accident. David Hilmers became his replacement.

Secondary payloads aboard Discovery were 12 Get Away Special canisters containing a variety of American and international experiments. The STS-42 Spacelab mission lasted eight days, completed 129 revolutions of Earth and travelled 2.9 million miles (4.7 million kilometres).

STS-45

CREW

Charles F. Bolden Jr – Commander
Brian Duffy – Pilot
Kathryn D. Sullivan – Mission Specialist
David C. Leestma – Mission Specialist
C. Michael Foale – Mission Specialist
Byron K. Lichtenberg – Payload Specialist
Dirk D. Frimout – Payload Specialist (ESA)

SPACECRAFT

Atlantis, OV-104

LAUNCH DATE

24 March 1992

MISSION

• Atmospheric Laboratory for Applications and
  Science-1 (ATLAS-1).

The primary non-deployable payload for this mission was the Atmospheric Laboratory for Applications and Science (ATLAS-1), namechecked in bold blue letters at the bottom of the mission patch. The Earth and Sun are the focus of the design, as the ATLAS-1 module – containing experiments from the USA and elsewhere – was used to observe the Sun and planet Earth extensively. The mission objectives were to conduct studies in atmospheric chemistry, solar radiation, space-plasma physics and ultraviolet astronomy. In the artwork, Atlantis can be seen reaching a high-inclination orbit after launching from the Kennedy Space Center, as indicated by the stylized red trajectory. From this position in orbit, the ATLAS-1 laboratory could best view Earth, the Sun and the surrounding environment. The crew members are named around the edge of the patch, and a lone star (bottom left) is a tribute to backup payload specialists Michael Lampton and Charles Chappell and to all who worked on the mission.

The shuttle crew also conducted the Shuttle Solar Backscatter Ultraviolet experiment (SSBUV), one Get Away Special experiment and six additional mid-deck experiments. The mission lasted nine days and completed 143 revolutions of Earth.

DID YOU KNOW?
By the time Atlantis touched down, the STS-45 crew had travelled 3.2 million miles (5.2 million kilometres).

Left to right: (back) Byron Lichtenberg, Michael Foale, David Leestma, Kathryn Sullivan, Dirk Frimout; (front) Brian Duffy, Charles Bolden

CREW

Daniel C. Brandenstein – Commander
Kevin P. Chilton – Pilot
Kathryn C. Thornton – Mission Specialist
Richard J. Hieb – Mission Specialist
Thomas D. Akers – Mission Specialist
Bruce E. Melnick – Mission Specialist
Pierre J. Thuot – Mission Specialist

SPACECRAFT

Endeavour, OV-105

LAUNCH DATE

7 May 1992

MISSION

- First flight of Space Shuttle Endeavour.
- Retrieval, repair and deployment Intelsat 603 satellite (also known as Intelsat VI F-3).

Left to right: Kathryn Thornton, Bruce Melnick,
Pierre Thuot, Daniel Brandenstein, Kevin Chilton,
Thomas Akers, Richard Hieb

STS-49 was the maiden flight of Endeavour, the newest orbiter in the Space Transportation System fleet and the last ever to be built. The large sailing ship in the centre of the patch is HMS *Endeavour*, the 18th-century Royal Navy vessel commanded by the explorer Captain James Cook on his famous scientific voyages to the uncharted waters of the Pacific Ocean. The insignia honours HMS *Endeavour*'s historical expeditions while celebrating the first flight of Space Shuttle Endeavour and its quest to continue space exploration into the future. The small stars set against the blue background recall the US flag as well as waves in the ocean. The flags flying from the ship's masts represent the schools that won the contest to name NASA's new shuttle Endeavour (blue and yellow – Senatobia Middle School, Mississippi; green and white – Tallulah Falls School, Georgia). The artwork was produced by graphic artist Sean Collins with creative guidance from the crew.

The primary objective for STS-49 was the retrieval, repair and redeployment of the Intelsat 603 satellite, which had been left dormant in space since its launch on board a Titan rocket in 1990. A series of EVAs were performed by the mission specialists to capture the satellite and install a new perigee kick motor to propel it into a geosynchronous Earth orbit.

CREW

Richard N. Richards – Commander
Kenneth D. Bowersox – Pilot
Bonnie J. Dunbar – Mission Specialist
Ellen S. Baker – Mission Specialist
Carl J. Meade – Mission Specialist
Lawrence J. DeLucas – Payload Specialist
Eugene H. Trinh – Payload Specialist

SPACECRAFT

Columbia, OV-102

LAUNCH DATE

25 June 1992

MISSION

- Spacelab mission.
- United States Microgravity Laboratory-1.
- First Extended Duration Orbiter flight.

Designed by the crew of Columbia, the STS-50 patch focuses on the microgravity-science objectives of the mission, using the United States Microgravity Laboratory-1 (USML-1) carried inside Columbia's payload bay. The large letters USML extend out of the orbiter's payload bay while the shuttle orbits Earth vertically, an orientation typical of microgravity research and also resembling the number 1 in the name USML-1. The laboratory is shown inside Columbia's payload bay with the microgravity symbol µg clearly marked. STS-50 was the first Extended Duration Orbiter (EDO) flight of the Space Shuttle Program, and visible below the USML-1 module inside Columbia's payload bay is the EDO pallet. The US flag within the letters USML and the green-highlighted landmass of the USA celebrate the all-American science mission. The large USML extends beyond the boundaries of the mission patch, suggesting the expansion of knowledge in microgravity research.

The extended microgravity mission contributed to research on longer-duration stays in space, so paving the way for later space-station operations. The USML-1 carried 31 microgravity experiments in five different categories: fluid dynamics, crystal growth, combustion science, biological science and technology demonstration.

Left to right: Ellen Baker, Kenneth Bowersox, Bonnie Dunbar, Richard Richards, Carl Meade, Eugene Trinh, Lawrence DeLucas

CREW

Loren J. Shriver – Commander
Andrew M. Allen – Pilot
Jeffrey A. Hoffman – Mission Specialist
Franklin R. Chang-Díaz – Mission Specialist
Claude Nicollier – Mission Specialist (ESA)
Marsha S. Ivins – Mission Specialist
Franco Malerba – Payload Specialist (ASI)

SPACECRAFT

Atlantis, OV-104

LAUNCH DATE

31 July 1992

MISSION

Deployment of European Retrievable Carrier (EURECA).
Operation of the Tethered Satellite System (TSS).

STS-46 was a collaboration between NASA, the Italian Space Agency (ASI) and the European Space Agency (ESA), and the national flags of the USA and Italy are shown either side of the ESA insignia at the bottom of the patch. The ESA's European Retrievable Carrier (EURECA) satellite, shown on the right of the patch, orbits Earth with its solar panels extended after deployment from Atlantis. The centre of the patch illustrates the joint NASA/ASI Tethered Satellite System (TSS) leaving the shuttle's payload bay. To the left of the TSS, a purple spiral emanates from an electron generator within the bay, illustrating how the TSS will investigate electromagnetic interactions between the tether/satellite/orbiter system and the ambient space plasma environment. The USA, Italy and much of Europe are visible in the scene below.

The EURECA satellite, with 15 on-board experiments, was deployed from STS-46 and left in Earth orbit. It was retrieved 11 months later during STS-57 and returned to Earth for evaluation. The mission lasted eight days and covered a distance of 3.3 million miles (5.3 million kilometres).

DID YOU KNOW?

The Tethered Satellite System (TSS) was intended to travel 12½ miles (20.1 kilometres) from the shuttle during the STS-57 mission, but the tether became jammed and the TSS reached only 840 feet (256 meters) before returning to Atlantis.

Left to right: (back) Marsha Ivins, Claude Nicollier,
Jeffrey Hoffman, Franklin Chang-Díaz, Franco Malerba;
(front) Andrew Allen, Loren Shriver

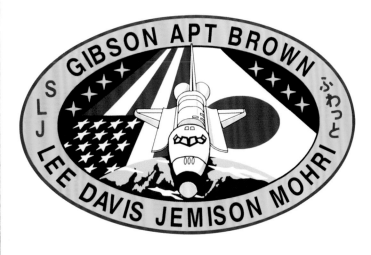

CREW

Robert L. 'Hoot' Gibson – Commander
Curtis L. Brown Jr – Pilot
Mark C. Lee – Mission Specialist
N. Jan Davis – Mission Specialist
Jerome 'Jay' Apt – Mission Specialist
Mae C. Jemison – Mission Specialist
Mamoru Mohri – Payload Specialist (NASDA)

SPACECRAFT

Endeavour, OV-105

LAUNCH DATE

12 September 1992

MISSION

• Joint Spacelab-J mission with NASDA/JAXA.

The STS-47 mission-patch design was a joint effort between the crew members, just as the mission itself was a joint venture between the USA and Japan. The primary payload was the Spacelab-J science laboratory, developed by NASA and the National Space Development Agency of Japan (NASDA). Endeavour is featured in the centre of the insignia with Spacelab-J inside its payload bay. The two national flags sit side-by-side behind the orbiter to acknowledge the collaborative effort of both nations in the pursuit of scientific research into microgravity. Alaska and Japan are visible at the bottom of the patch, emphasizing the 57-degree high-inclination orbit in which the shuttle would operate. The red Latin letters on the left stand for Spacelab-J, while the red Japanese characters spell *fuwatto* (weightlessness), in recognition of the microgravity nature of the mission.

The purpose of the Spacelab-J laboratory was to conduct microgravity research into life sciences and materials sciences, with 24 materials science and 20 life sciences experiments performed. Of these, 35 were sponsored by NASDA, seven by NASA and two were joint efforts by both space agencies.

DID YOU KNOW?
STS-47 carried the first married couple (Mark Lee and Jan Davis) and the first African-American woman (Mae Jemison) into space, while Mamoru Mohri became the first Japanese astronaut to fly on board the shuttle.

Left to right: (back) Jan Davis, Mark Lee, Hoot Gibson, Mae Jemison, Mamoru Mohri; (front) Jay Apt, Curtis Brown

STS-52

STS-52

CREW

James D. Wetherbee – Commander
Michael A. Baker – Pilot
Charles L. Veach – Mission Specialist
William M. Shepherd – Mission Specialist
Tamara E. Jernigan – Mission Specialist
Steven G. MacLean – Payload Specialist (CSA)

SPACECRAFT

Columbia, OV-102

LAUNCH DATE

22 October 1992

MISSION

• Deployment of Laser Geodynamic Satellite
  (LAGEOS II).
• United States Microgravity Payload-1 (USMP-1).

Left to right: (back) Michael Baker, James Wetherbee,
Steven MacLean; (front) Charles Veach, Tamara Jernigan,
William Shepherd

With NASA's ever expanding presence among the stars as the frontiers of space exploration advance, the STS-52 mission insignia is dominated by a large golden-yellow star – the star being a symbol often associated with the frontier days of the American Wild West. The bold red arrowhead placed over the star is in the form of the Greek letter lambda to reflect the laser measurements recorded by the Laser Geodynamic Satellite (LAGEOS II) and the Lambda Point Experiment included in the United States Microgravity Payload (USMP-1). The orbiter Columbia is in the centre of the patch, with its payload-bay doors open and the Remote Manipulator System robotic arm, also known as Canadarm, reaching out of the shuttle. The Canadarm is shown with a red maple leaf to represent the mission's Canadian payload specialist Steven MacLean. The background shows a cloudy Earth and a series of constellations in the sky.

LAGEOS II is a joint project by NASA and the Italian Space Agency (ASI) to study Earth's tectonic plates. The USMP-1 facility consisted of three microgravity experiments within Columbia's payload bay. These were the Lambda Point Experiment, the Space Acceleration Measurement System (SAMS) and the French MEPHISTO experiment (*Matérial pour l'Étude des Phénomènes Interessant la Solidification sur Terre et en Orbite*, which translates as 'Materials for the Study of Interesting Phenomena of Solidification on Earth and in Orbit').

CREW

David M. Walker – Commander
Robert D. Cabana – Pilot
Guion S. 'Guy' Bluford Jr – Mission Specialist
James S. Voss – Mission Specialist
Michael R. Clifford – Mission Specialist

SPACECRAFT

Discovery, OV-103

LAUNCH DATE

2 December 1992

MISSION

• Final classified Department of Defense mission.

The patch for STS-53 is pentagonal in shape, recalling the headquarters of the US Department of Defense. This design was chosen in recognition of the support given to the Space Shuttle Program by the department over several missions. Discovery is featured blasting upwards and breaking through the frame of the patch on its way into space as the programme continues to push the boundaries of space exploration. The orange rocket trail is an astronaut emblem, to represent the gold badge that every astronaut receives once they have flown into space. At the bottom of the artwork, a US flag displays five stars and three stripes in reference to the mission's designated number, 53, and highlights the USA's position at the forefront of space exploration. The colours of the sky and on the thin band along the edge of the flag represent the various military backgrounds of the crew: Navy, Marine Corps, Army and Air Force.

This final classified Department of Defense mission lasted seven days. Two unclassified secondary payloads were also on board, as well as a series of unclassified experiments.

Left to right: (back) David Walker, Robert Cabana, Michael Clifford; (front) Guy Bluford, James Voss

STS-54

CREW

John H. Casper – Commander
Donald R. McMonagle – Pilot
Mario Runco Jr – Mission Specialist
Gregory J. Harbaugh – Mission Specialist
Susan J. Helms – Mission Specialist

SPACECRAFT

Endeavour, OV-105

LAUNCH DATE

13 January 1993

MISSION

- Deployment of Tracking and Data Relay Satellite-F (TDRS-F).
- Diffuse X-Ray Spectrometer (DXS).

Left to right: Mario Runco, John Casper,
Donald McMonagle, Susan Helms, Gregory Harbaugh

On this bold and patriotic mission patch – created by graphic artist Sean Collins and the crew – Endeavour is replaced by a soaring American bald eagle. The eagle was chosen because the shuttle, like the eagle, is an icon of the USA and a source of national pride. As the bird triumphantly swoops down with its wings fully extended, we can see a large star gripped tightly in its talons. This is for the Tracking and Data Relay Satellite-F (TDRS-F) that was carried into space by Endeavour on this mission. This was the fifth TDRS to be placed into orbit, and the previous four are represented by the smaller stars in the border. The secondary payload was the Diffuse X-Ray Spectrometer (DXS), which gathered data on X-ray radiation from diffuse sources in the universe, and the starless space in the background is a reference to that function. North America is clearly visible on the radiant blue Earth, which serves as a reminder that the research-oriented and scientific nature of the mission will benefit the USA and all humanity. The cloudy planet is also a reference to the crew's task of photographing the planet as part of NASA's Mission to Planet Earth (MTPE) programme, dedicated to studying Earth and the effects of natural and human-induced changes in the environment.

TDRS-F was deployed on the first day of the mission. Mission specialists Mario Runco and Gregory Harbaugh went on to perform an EVA that lasted almost five hours in which they carried out a series of tasks within the shuttle's payload bay, demonstrating the challenges and effectiveness of working in space.

CREW

Kenneth D. Cameron – Commander
Stephen S. Oswald – Pilot
C. Michael Foale – Mission Specialist
Kenneth D. Cockrell – Mission Specialist
Ellen L. Ochoa – Mission Specialist

SPACECRAFT

Discovery, OV-103

LAUNCH DATE

8 April 1993

MISSION

- Atmospheric Laboratory for Applications and Science-2 (ATLAS-2).
- Deployment of SPARTAN 201.

The STS-56 insignia illustrates the objectives of the mission as it would be seen from the crew's perspective. The primary payload was the Atmospheric Laboratory for Applications and Science-2 (ATLAS-2), designed to accumulate data on how Earth's middle atmosphere is affected by solar activity. This vibrant design depicts Discovery's payload bay revealing the ATLAS-2, which contained the Shuttle Solar Backscatter Ultra Violet (SSBUV) experiment, as well as the SPARTAN 201, which carried two telescopes to study the Sun's atmosphere and the solar wind. Featured prominently in the artwork are Earth and the Sun, the two main areas of investigation for this mission as part of NASA's Mission to Planet Earth (MTPE) programme. Earth's atmosphere is shown as a visible spectrum with the stylized solar corona stretching across the blackness of space.

This was the second flight of the ATLAS science laboratory, which had been flown a year earlier on STS-45. The Remote Manipulator System robotic arm was used to deploy the SPARTAN 201 three days into the mission. On 17 April, it was retrieved and safely stored in Discovery's payload bay, ready for its data to be analysed back on Earth.

Left to right: Kenneth Cockrell, Stephen Oswald, Michael Foale, Kenneth Cameron, Ellen Ochoa

CREW

Steven R. Nagel – Commander
Terence T. 'Tom' Henricks – Pilot
Jerry L. Ross – Mission Specialist
Charles J. Precourt – Mission Specialist
Bernard A. Harris Jr – Mission Specialist
Ulrich Walter – Payload Specialist (DFVLR)
Hans W. Schlegel – Payload Specialist (DFVLR)

SPACECRAFT

Columbia, OV-102

LAUNCH DATE

26 April 1993

MISSION

• Spacelab D-2 payload operated by Germany.

Left to right: (back) Bernard Harris, Hans Schlegel,
Jerry Ross, Ulrich Walter; (front) Tom Henricks,
Steven Nagel, Charles Precourt

STS-55 was the second joint American and German mission to carry the Spacelab science facility, and as well as the NASA designation, the mission is also known as D-2 (Deutschland 2) as shown at the top of the mission patch. Columbia is at the centre of the design with its payload-bay doors wide open exposing the Spacelab facility, while the rainbow trail symbolizes both the shuttle's trajectory and hopes for a brighter future through the scientific research and knowledge obtained from the on-board experiments and investigations. Each star is for one of the astronauts' children and thus the legacy of the Space Shuttle Program for future generations. The crew members' names are displayed around the grey border, and the two backup payload specialists who never flew on the mission (Gerhard Thiele and Renate Brümmer) are acknowledged by the two blue stars. The national flags of the USA and Germany are featured on the right-hand side of the patch, which was designed with creative input from all crew members.

The German-led Spacelab D-2 mission consisted of 88 experiments from different nations across the globe. The areas of study were materials and life sciences, technology applications, observations of Earth, astronomy and atmospheric physics.

STS-57

CREW

Ronald J. Grabe – Commander
Brian Duffy – Pilot
G. David Low – Payload Commander
Nancy J. Sherlock – Mission Specialist
Peter J. K. 'Jeff' Wisoff – Mission Specialist
Janice E. Voss – Mission Specialist

SPACECRAFT

Endeavour, OV-105

LAUNCH DATE

21 June 1993

MISSION

- SPACEHAB-1 mission.
- Retrieval of European Retrievable Carrier (EURECA).

The crew members of STS-57 worked with artist Tim Hall to create this colourful mission patch. The inner red border replicates the distinctive cross-section profile of the SPACEHAB facility, which can also be seen inside the payload bay of Endeavour as it soars over Earth, leaving a red trajectory behind it. The European Retrieval Carrier (EURECA) is illustrated above the shuttle, ready to be captured by the Remote Manipulator System (RMS) robotic arm. The yellow plumes and five orange stars trailing EURECA recall the astronaut badge, which every NASA astronaut receives. The five orange stars along with the 7-shape formed by the RMS robotic arm also give us the mission number, 57. The six crew members are acknowledged by the six stars in the US flag at the top of the insignia.

SPACEHAB was a pressurized science laboratory designed to increase the workspace for experimentation during the ten-day mission. In all, 22 biomedical and materials-sciences experiments were conducted. The EURECA satellite had been deployed a year earlier on STS-46 and was host to a range of experiments studying the long-term effects of microgravity. EURECA was captured on 24 June, but its antennae failed to retract. Astronauts David Low and Jeff Wisoff performed a spacewalk to fold down the unresponsive antennae manually, after which the spacecraft was stowed in the payload bay for its return to Earth.

Left to right: Jeff Wisoff, Brian Duffy, Nancy Sherlock, Janice Voss, Ronald Grabe, David Low

CREW

Frank L. Culbertson Jr – Commander
William F. Readdy – Pilot
James H. Newman – Mission Specialist
Daniel W. Bursch – Mission Specialist
Carl E. Walz – Mission Specialist

SPACECRAFT

Discovery, OV-103

LAUNCH DATE

12 September 1993

MISSION

- Deployment of Advanced Communications Technology Satellite (ACTS).
- Deployment of Orbiting and Retrievable Far and Extreme Ultraviolet Spectrograph-Shuttle Pallet Satellite (ORFEUS-SPAS).

Left to right: Frank Culbertson, Daniel Bursch, Carl Walz, William Readdy, James Newman

In the artwork for STS-51, Discovery is depicted high above Earth, suspended in space, with a double spiral of the US flag trailing behind it. The interweaving spirals suggest the coming together of men and women across the nation to strengthen America's commitment to space exploration and expansion. The five stars in the flag are for the crew and join with the single gold star to give us the mission's designated number, 51. The gold star represents one of the mission's primary payloads, the Advanced Communications Technology Satellite (ACTS). The rays emanating from it illustrate the advanced communication technologies that ACTS will provide in orbit. The secondary payload was the German-sponsored Orbiting and Retrievable Far and Extreme Ultraviolet Spectrograph-Shuttle Pallet Satellite (ORFEUS-SPAS), depicted by the arrow-shaped object on the right of the patch in the colours of the German flag. The ORFEUS-SPAS was designed to investigate celestial objects, represented here by the constellation Orion, the seven stars of which are also a tribute to the brave astronauts who lost their lives on STS-51-L.

During the ten-day mission, mission specialists James Newman and Carl Walz performed a seven-hour EVA testing tools, tethers and foot restraints that would be used on the upcoming Hubble Space Telescope servicing mission, STS-61.

CREW

John E. Blaha – Commander
Richard A. Searfoss – Pilot
M. Rhea Seddon – Payload Commander
William S. McArthur – Mission Specialist
David A. Wolf – Mission Specialist
Shannon W. Lucid – Mission Specialist
Martin J. Fettman – Payload Specialist

SPACECRAFT

Columbia, OV-102

LAUNCH DATE

18 October 1993

MISSION

• Spacelab Life Sciences-2 mission (SLS-2).

STS-58 was the second Spacelab mission in the Space Shuttle Program dedicated to life sciences. Designed by the crew of Columbia, the mission patch focuses heavily on the biological studies to be conducted during the mission. The hexagonal shape comes from the carbon ring, a molecule common in all living organisms. The astronauts' names run around the edge along with a medical caduceus on the left and a veterinary caduceus on the right that represent the life-science experiments at the heart of the mission. The Spacelab Life Sciences-2 (SLS-2) facility is clearly visible inside the shuttle's payload bay. Encircling the central image is the double helix of the DNA molecule found in all life forms. The yellow within the double helix suggests the energy source required for life on Earth: the Sun. STS-58 lasted for two weeks and required the use of the Extended Duration Orbiter (EDO) pallet, visible at the back of Columbia's payload bay. The design was conceived by pilot Rick Searfoss with creative input from the whole crew.

DID YOU KNOW?

Six rats were killed and dissected on STS-58, which caused controversy. The experiments were designed to gain vital knowledge of the effects of microgravity on tissue samples while still in space and without the potential for the samples to be affected by gravity if studied back on Earth.

Left to right: (back) John Blaha, William McArthur, Martin Fettman; (front) David Wolf, Shannon Lucid, Rhea Seddon, Richard Searfoss

STS-61

CREW

Richard O. Covey – Commander
Kenneth D. Bowersox – Pilot
F. Story Musgrave – Payload Commander
Kathryn C. Thornton – Mission Specialist
Claude Nicollier – Mission Specialist (ESA)
Jeffrey A. Hoffman – Mission Specialist
Thomas D. Akers – Mission Specialist

SPACECRAFT

Endeavour, OV-105

LAUNCH DATE

2 December 1993

MISSION

• First Hubble Space Telescope servicing mission.

Left to right: (back) Richard Covey, Jeffrey Hoffman,
Thomas Akers; (front) Kenneth Bowersox, Kathryn Thornton,
Story Musgrave, Claude Nicollier

STS-61 was the first mission to service the Hubble Space Telescope. The patch is dominated by a large gold astronaut emblem emanating from Earth and ascending high towards the stars, acknowledging the many people from all over the globe who work tirelessly to contribute to the common goal of expanding our knowledge of the solar system and beyond. The two circles represent the optical configuration of Hubble, where light is focused by reflections from a large primary mirror and a smaller secondary mirror. After the successful repair operation, Hubble went on to provide a wealth of new knowledge and astounding high-resolution images of distant stars, galaxies and nebulae in the far reaches of the universe, as well as surveying our own solar system. The shuttle is featured proudly racing towards the star of the astronaut emblem as a reminder of its critical role in discovering the mysteries of deep space.

The mission to service Hubble was one of most challenging and complex missions ever performed in space. After the deployment of Hubble three years earlier on STS-31, a small but significant flaw was discovered with its primary mirror, which caused images to be blurred. During a series of EVAs, astronauts carried out routine maintenance and performed complex tasks to install the specially designed optical components to correct Hubble's vision.

CREW

Charles F. Bolden Jr – Commander
Kenneth S. Reightler Jr – Pilot
N. Jan Davis – Mission Specialist
Ronald M. Sega – Mission Specialist
Franklin R. Chang-Díaz – Mission Specialist
Sergei K. Krikalev – Mission Specialist (RKA)

SPACECRAFT

Discovery, OV-103

LAUNCH DATE

3 February 1994

MISSION

- SPACEHAB-2 mission.
- Wake Shield Facility-1 (WSF-1).
- First stage of the US/Russian Shuttle–
  Mir programme.

STS-60 signalled the beginning of a new era of US/Russian cooperation in human spaceflight. In a configuration that resembles the open wings of an eagle, the patch shows the two national flags proudly displayed together in a symbolic show of unity between the two space agencies. The names of the six crew members encircle the design, each with a star next to their name. Discovery is illustrated in orbit, payload-bay doors wide open, revealing the SPACEHAB-2 science facility towards the front and the 100th Get Away Special payload at the back. The Remote Manipulator System (RMS) robotic arm can be seen preparing to deploy Wake Shield Facility-1 (WSF-1).

SPACEHAB-2 was the second flight for the SPACEHAB pressurized module. Of the 12 experiments undertaken, four involved materials science, seven life sciences and one was to collect space dust. The WSF-1 was an experimental science platform designed to be retrievable by the crew, but the small spacecraft failed to deploy.

DID YOU KNOW?

The STS-60 mission was the first time a Russian cosmonaut had flown on board the Space Shuttle.

Left to right: (back) Ronald Sega, Sergei Krikalev; (middle) Franklin Chang-Díaz, Jan Davis; (front) Kenneth Reightler, Charles Bolden

CREW

John H. Casper – Commander
Andrew M. Allen – Pilot
Pierre J. Thuot – Mission Specialist
Charles D. Gemar – Mission Specialist
Marsha S. Ivins – Mission Specialist

SPACECRAFT

Columbia, OV-102

LAUNCH DATE

4 March 1994

MISSION

• United States Microgravity Payload-2 (USMP-2).
• Office of Aeronautics and Space Technology-2 (OAST-2).

Left to right: (back) Charles Gemar, Marsha Ivins, Pierre Thuot; (front) Andrew Allen, John Casper

With creative input from the crew, this beautiful artwork for the STS-62 patch was designed by former NASA research pilot and artist Mark Pestana. The arrow-head shape with the point facing up represents America's continued commitment to reaching new heights in human spaceflight. In preparation for re-entry into Earth's atmosphere, Columbia is depicted in the correct entry-interface attitude. The multi-coloured horizon symbolizes the diverse scientific studies uniting for this mission, while the sunrise points to a brighter future for generations to come through today's research in space.

With the United States Microgravity Payload-2 (USMP-2) and the Office of Aeronautics and Space Technology-2 (OAST-2) on board, the experiments undertaken during the mission covered a vast range of scientific investigations into the effects of microgravity. USMP-2 conducted five experiments concerning crystal growth in microgravity and materials processing, while OAST-2 ran six experiments focusing on spaceflight technology.

CREW

Sidney M. Gutierrez – Commander
Kevin P. Chilton – Pilot
Linda M. Godwin – Mission Specialist
Jerome 'Jay' Apt – Mission Specialist
Michael R. Clifford – Mission Specialist
Thomas D. Jones – Mission Specialist

SPACECRAFT

Endeavour, OV-105

LAUNCH DATE

9 April 1994

MISSION

• Space Radar Laboratory (SRL-1).

STS-59 was part of NASA's Mission to Planet Earth programme, which was established to conduct studies and extensive surveys of Earth's landmass and atmosphere. This Space Radar Laboratory-1 (SRL-1) mission patch features a nod to the gold astronaut badge awarded to NASA astronauts once they have flown in space. The gold emblem projecting down onto Earth from the shuttle's payload bay represents the three operating wavelengths of the on-board Spaceborne Imaging Radar-C/X-Band Synthetic Aperture Radar (SIR-C/X-SAR) as it collects valuable information about our planet's surface. SRL-1 also contained the Measurement of Air Pollution from Satellites (MAPS) instrument, which was used to study Earth's atmosphere. The badge is a reminder of the importance of human spaceflight in the pursuit of a greater understanding of our planet. A star-filled space scene acknowledges the many people from around the world who have contributed to the success of the SRL-1 mission and the Mission to Planet Earth programme. Artist Mark Pestana designed the insignia.

The project was the result of the combined efforts of over 100 scientists in 13 countries. SRL-1 surveyed more than 400 sites during the 11-day mission, including 19 primary observation sites in Brazil, Michigan, North Carolina and Europe. Endeavour also tested some improved heat-shield tiles during the flight with several new tiles being added to the shuttle's thermal-protection system.

Left to right: (back) Kevin Chilton, Sidney Gutierrez; (middle) Linda Godwin, Michael Clifford; (front) Thomas Jones, Jay Apt

STS-65

CREW

Robert D. Cabana – Commander
James D. Halsell Jr – Pilot
Richard J. Hieb – Mission Specialist
Carl E. Walz – Mission Specialist
Leroy Chiao – Mission Specialist
Donald A. Thomas – Mission Specialist
Chiaki Mukai – Payload Specialist (NASDA)

SPACECRAFT

Columbia, OV-102

LAUNCH DATE

8 July 1994

MISSION

• Spacelab mission. International Microgravity
  Laboratory-2.

Left to right: (back) Leroy Chiao, James Halsell,
Chiaki Mukai, Carl Walz; (front): Richard Hieb,
Robert Cabana, Donald Thomas

The STS-65 mission patch features two yellow stars shooting upwards into space with IML in bold red letters across the front announcing that this is the second International Microgravity Laboratory mission, IML-2. Columbia can be seen orbiting the central logo and soaring through space with its payload-bay doors open exposing the Spacelab module inside. This international scientific research mission focused on life sciences, materials-processing experiments and the effects of microgravity. The names of the six crew members on the 15-day spaceflight are displayed around the inner edge of the patch. The artwork was produced by artist Sean Collins with creative direction from the crew.

During the spaceflight, the crew of Columbia took time to remember the 25th anniversary of the first lunar landing on Apollo 11. Fittingly, the Command Module that carried the Apollo 11 crew to the Moon and back was also named Columbia.

DID YOU KNOW?

On STS-65, astronaut Chiaka Mukai became the first Japanese woman in space, representing the Japanese space agency NASDA (JAXA from 2003). Mukai flew two shuttle flights, STS-65 and STS-95.

CREW

Richard N. Richards – Commander
L. Blaine Hammond Jr – Pilot
Jerry M. Linenger – Mission Specialist
Susan J. Helms – Mission Specialist
Carl J. Meade – Mission Specialist
Mark C. Lee – Mission Specialist

SPACECRAFT

Discovery, OV-103

LAUNCH DATE

9 September 1994

MISSION

- Lidar In-space Technology Experiment (LITE).
- Deployment of SPARTAN-201.

The primary payload for STS-64 was the Lidar In-space Technology Experiment (LITE), which uses a lidar (light detection and ranging) laser-pulse system to study Earth's atmosphere. The STS-64 mission patch sees Discovery in orbit, projecting three gold laser beams towards Earth's atmosphere to represent the three operating wavelengths of LITE. The three beams, the gold ring and the star at the top also make up the NASA astronaut emblem. The shuttle's Remote Manipulator System robotic arm is shown ready to deploy SPARTAN-201, an experiment consisting of two telescopes that would investigate the Sun's atmosphere and solar-wind activity. Two astronauts (Lee and Meade) are shown performing EVA duties to test the Simplified Aid for EVA Rescue (SAFER), a new propulsive backpack designed to be used in the event that an astronaut becomes untethered. Encircling the patch are the names of the crew, each of which has a star either side of their name. The crew members with a background in the US Navy have gold stars and those from the US Air Force have blue.

LITE was part of NASA's Mission to Planet Earth programme, and it collected more than 43 hours of valuable data. Teams from 20 countries participated in verifying data gathered from LITE. The mission lasted 11 days, and the shuttle completed 176 revolutions of Earth.

Left to right: (back) Mark Lee, Jerry Linenger, Carl Meade; (front) Blaine Hammond, Richard Richards, Susan Helms

CREW

Michael A. Baker – Commander
Terrence W. Wilcutt – Pilot
Thomas D. Jones – Payload Commander
Steven L. Smith – Mission Specialist
Daniel W. Bursch – Mission Specialist
Peter J. K. 'Jeff' Wisoff – Mission Specialist

SPACECRAFT

Endeavour, OV-105

LAUNCH DATE

30 September 1994

MISSION

• Space Radar Laboratory (SRL-2).

A pseudocylindrical map of Earth in blue and black forms the central motif of the patch for STS-68, which was part of NASA's Mission to Planet Earth programme. We see Endeavour orbiting Earth, while the characters SRL2 outlined in red span the width and height of the globe to indicate the worldwide coverage of the Space Radar Laboratory-2 mission. The primary payload on board Endeavour was the Spaceborne Imaging Radar-C/X-Band Synthetic Aperture Radar (SIR-C/X-SAR), which gathered valuable information about Earth's landmass. SRL-2 also housed the Measurement of Air Pollution from Satellites (MAPS) instrument, designed to study Earth's atmosphere, which is symbolized by the gold border of the patch. The red, blue and black colour scheme represents the three operating wavelengths of the SIR-C/X-SAR. The small shuttle alone in space orbiting the huge Earth shows how vital a role the Space Shuttle Program plays in the exploration of our own planet. Germany and Italy partnered with the USA for this mission, and their national flags appear in the border along with the Stars and Stripes. Artist Sean Collins created the piece with creative guidance from the crew.

STS-68 marked the second flight of the Space Radar Laboratory, which allowed scientists to compare the findings of both missions. The crew conducted other experiments during the flight, including two sponsored by university student groups and one by the Swedish Space Corporation.

Left to right: (back) Michael Baker, Terrence Wilcutt; (front) Thomas Jones, Jeff Wisoff, Steven Smith, Daniel Bursch

STS-66

CREW

Donald R. McMonagle – Commander
Curtis L. Brown Jr – Pilot
Ellen L. Ochoa – Payload Commander
Joseph R. Tanner – Mission Specialist
Jean-François Clervoy – Mission Specialist (ESA)
Scott E. Parazynski – Mission Specialist

SPACECRAFT

Atlantis, OV-104

LAUNCH DATE

3 November 1994

MISSION

- Atmospheric Laboratory for Applications and Science-3 (ATLAS-3).
- Deployment and retrieval of CRISTA-SPAS-01.

The mission-patch artwork for STS-66 features Atlantis launching into space for another scientific research mission in NASA's Mission to Planet Earth programme. The fiery plumes trailing the shuttle form part of the gold astronaut badge emblem used so often in Space Shuttle Program insignias. A primary non-deployable payload on this mission was the Atmospheric Laboratory for Applications and Science-3 (ATLAS-3), which carried experiments for the study of the composition of Earth's middle atmosphere and the effects caused by the Sun, as depicted in the artwork by the blazing Sun peering out over the visible spectrum of the atmosphere. The second primary payload was the Cryogenic Infrared Spectrometers and Telescopes for the Atmosphere-Shuttle Pallet Satellite (CRISTA-SPAS), which was deployed from the shuttle and orbited Earth gathering vital data on the chemical composition of Earth's middle atmosphere. The distinctive shape of the CRISTA-SPAS is illustrated orbiting Earth to the left of Atlantis.

The mission lasted 11 days, completed 174 revolutions of Earth and travelled 4.5 million miles (7.25 million kilometres). The CRISTA-SPAS was retrieved and stowed in the payload bay of Atlantis and the crew returned with a wealth of scientific data for scientists all over the world to analyse.

Left to right: Jean-François Clervoy, Scott Parazynski, Curtis Brown, Joseph Tanner, Donald McMonagle, Ellen Ochoa

STS-63

CREW

James D. Wetherbee – Commander
Eileen M. Collins – Pilot
Bernard A. Harris Jr – Payload Commander
C. Michael Foale – Mission Specialist
Janice E. Voss – Mission Specialist
Vladimir G. Titov – Mission Specialist (RKA)

SPACECRAFT

Discovery, OV-103

LAUNCH DATE

3 February 1995

MISSION

- SPACEHAB-3.
- First approach and flyaround of Russian Mir space station.
- First female shuttle pilot.

Left to right: (back) Bernard Harris, Michael Foale; (front) Janice Voss, Eileen Collins, James Wetherbee, Vladimir Titov

The STS-63 crew patch illustrates Discovery manoeuvring to perform the first rendezvous with Russia's Mir space station as part of the joint US/Russian Shuttle–Mir programme. The name Mir, which translates as 'peace', is written in red Cyrillic letters on the side of the space station. As Discovery approaches while orbiting Earth, the SPACEHAB-3 pressurised science module can be seen at front of the payload bay along with the SPARTAN-204, a free-flying payload that analysed cosmic dust clouds. The six solar flares and three white stars represent the mission's designated number: 63. The crew names encircle the patch in blue and gold, recalling the military backgrounds of commander James Wetherbee (US Navy) and pilot Eileen Collins (US Air Force). The national flags of the USA and Russia sit side by side at the bottom of the insignia as a sign of the cooperation of the two nations on this historic rendezvous in space.

As well as Discovery rendezvousing with Mir for the first time, STS-63 carried the SPACEHAB-3 module containing an array of experiments in various scientific fields including biology and technology.

DID YOU KNOW?

On STS-63, Eileen M. Collins became the first female astronaut to pilot the shuttle; she also became the first female shuttle commander on STS-93 and flew on four shuttle flights in total.

CREW

Stephen S. Oswald – Commander
William G. Gregory – Pilot
Tamara E. Jernigan – Payload Commander
John M. Grunsfeld – Mission Specialist
Wendy B. Lawrence – Mission Specialist
Samuel T. Durrance – Payload Specialist
Ronald A. Parise – Payload Specialist

SPACECRAFT

Endeavour, OV-105

LAUNCH DATE

2 March 1995

MISSION

• ASTRO-2, consisting of three ultraviolet telescopes.

On the STS-67 mission patch, we see Endeavour orbiting Earth with the ASTRO-2 mounted onto the Instrument Pointing System in the payload bay. The three sets of rays emanating from the ASTRO-2 are for the three ultraviolet telescopes it housed: the Hopkins Ultraviolet Telescope, the Ultraviolet Imaging Telescope and the Wisconsin Ultraviolet Photo-Polarimeter Experiment. The telescopes were aligned to study the same astronomical objects in space and are shown here focusing together on part of the NASA logo, which also forms the A in ASTRO-2. This honours all the teams at NASA who work behind the scenes to make the Space Shuttle Program successful and help achieve a greater understanding of the universe through astronomy. The two atoms in the border represent the search in the ultraviolet spectrum for the signature of primordial helium from the very early universe. The galaxy in the background along with Jupiter and its four moons (a total of six celestial objects) plus the seven large stars combine to form the mission's number: 67.

The mission conducted an array of experiments relating to biomedical science, including a study into a potential treatment for colon cancer.

DID YOU KNOW?

STS-67 was the first advertised shuttle mission to be connected to the internet. People from all over the world logged onto the official ASTRO-2 website to ask the crew questions as it orbited Earth.

Left to right: (back) Ronald Parise, Wendy Lawrence, John Grunsfeld, Samuel Durrance; (front) Stephen Oswald, Tamara Jernigan, William Gregory

119

STS-71

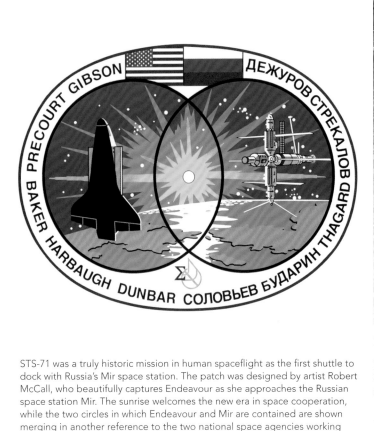

CREW

Robert L. 'Hoot' Gibson – Commander
Charles J. Precourt – Pilot
Ellen S. Baker – Mission Specialist
Gregory J. Harbaugh – Mission Specialist
Bonnie J. Dunbar – Mission Specialist
Anatoly Solovyev – Mir 'up' crew (RKA)
Nikolai Budarin – Mir 'up' crew (RKA)
Gennadi Strekalov – Mir 'down' crew (RKA)
Vladimir Dezhurov – Mir 'down' crew (RKA)
Norman E. Thagard – Mir 'down' crew

SPACECRAFT

Atlantis, OV-104

LAUNCH DATE

27 June 1995

MISSION

• First shuttle to dock with Russian Mir space station.

Left to right: (back) Norman Thagard, Gennadi Strekalov, Gregory Harbaugh, Ellen Baker, Charles Precourt, Bonnie Dunbar, Nikolai Budarin; (front) Vladimir Dezhurov, Hoot Gibson, Anatoly Solovyev

STS-71 was a truly historic mission in human spaceflight as the first shuttle to dock with Russia's Mir space station. The patch was designed by artist Robert McCall, who beautifully captures Endeavour as she approaches the Russian space station Mir. The sunrise welcomes the new era in space cooperation, while the two circles in which Endeavour and Mir are contained are shown merging in another reference to the two national space agencies working closely together. The flags of both nations are featured side by side at the top, again emphasizing the partnership. The mission control centres of both nations, who are responsible for the safety of their crews, are represented by the symbols at the bottom of the patch: the red sigma was used on the original NASA mission-control patch designed by Robert McCall. The names of the ten crew members *Endeavour* are to be found around the border.

During the five days Endeavour was docked with Mir, the crews conducted joint scientific investigations into biomedical science and microgravity using the Spacelab module inside Endeavour's payload bay.

DID YOU KNOW?

STS-71 was the 100th US manned space launch. While Endeavour was docked with Mir, it was the largest spacecraft ever to orbit Earth at that time and performed the first switch of a shuttle crew while in orbit.

CREW

Terence T. 'Tom' Henricks – Commander
Kevin R. Kregel – Pilot
Donald A. Thomas – Mission Specialist
Nancy J. Currie (née Sherlock) – Mission Specialist
Mary Ellen Weber – Mission Specialist

SPACECRAFT

Discovery, OV-103

LAUNCH DATE

13 July 1995

MISSION

- Deployment of Tracking and Data Relay Satellite-G (TDRS-G).

The primary objective of mission STS-70 was the deployment of NASA's Tracking and Data Relay Satellite-G (TDRS-G), the last in a series of satellites designed to provide communications and data transfer for spaceflights. The patch was designed by the crew, and it shows Discovery orbiting high above Earth. The three gold stars and the three points of the interwoven triangular ribbon are indicative of the unity TDRS provides between spacecraft, data and communications and Earth. The shape of the patch resembles that of the TDRS-G when stowed in the shuttle's payload bay.

During the remainder of the flight, once TDRS-G had been deployed, an array of experiments were conducted in biological sciences, protein crystal growth, chemistry and the dynamics of low-Earth orbit, microgravity eyesight investigations, and antibiotics research.

DID YOU KNOW?

Part of the STS-70 mission was the Shuttle Amateur Radio Experiment (SAREX), during which crew members communicated with radio operators on the ground.

Left to right: Kevin Kregel, Nancy J. Currie, Tom Henricks, Mary Ellen Weber, Donald; Thomas

CREW

David M. Walker – Commander
Kenneth D. Cockrell – Pilot
James S. Voss – Payload Commander
James H. Newman – Mission Specialist
Michael L. Gernhardt – Mission Specialist

SPACECRAFT

Endeavour, OV-105

LAUNCH DATE

7 September 1995

MISSION

- Deployment and retrieval of Wake Shield Facility-2 (WSF-2).
- Deployment and retrieval of SPARTAN 201-03.

Left to right: (back) Michael Gernhardt, James Newman, James Voss; (front) Kenneth Cockrell, David Walker

STS-69 was the first time two different payloads were deployed and retrieved on the same mission. To illustrate this, artist Mark Pestana shows Endeavour twice, both in launch configuration and in re-entry position. The two shuttles and their red spiral trajectories also add to the overall sense that the design resembles a spiral galaxy. The payloads were the Wake Shield Facility-2 (WSF-2), the SPARTAN 201-03, and the International Extreme Ultraviolet Hitchhiker (IEH-1). The WSF-2 is represented in the mission patch by the blue disc in the centre, which also features the astronaut emblem to stress the importance of human spaceflight. The constellations of Canis Major (bottom) and Canis Minor (top) acknowledge the skills and dedication of all personnel who contribute to the success of the Space Shuttle Program as well as highlighting the astronomical objectives of the SPARTAN 201-03 and International IEH-1. The SPARTAN and IEU-1 used X-ray, ultraviolet and visible-light instruments to study the Sun's atmosphere and galactic clusters.

STS-69 spent 11 days in space. Astronauts Voss and Gernhardt performed a six-hour spacewalk to evaluate various spacesuit modifications and to test techniques to be adopted on future International Space Station missions.

DID YOU KNOW?

Wake Shield Facility-2 (WSF-2) was deployed on the fifth day of the mission and became the first spacecraft to manoeuvre itself away from the shuttle by firing its own thruster.

CREW

Kenneth D. Bowersox – Commander
Kent V. Rominger – Pilot
Kathryn C. Thornton – Payload Commander
Catherine G. 'Cady' Coleman – Mission Specialist
Michael López-Alegría – Mission Specialist
Fred W. Leslie – Payload Specialist
Albert Sacco Jr – Payload Specialist

SPACECRAFT

Columbia, OV-102

LAUNCH DATE

20 October 1995

MISSION

• Spacelab mission.
• United States Microgravity Laboratory-2.

This design focuses on the mathematical, geometric and philosophical teachings and theories of the ancient Greeks. Plato and other philosophers including Pythagoras and Euclid investigated and verified that there are only five possible regular convex polyhedrons, later named the 'Platonic solids'. These are represented by the four symmetrical, three-dimensional objects (polyhedrons) at the bottom of the patch, and the shape of the insignia itself. Plato, and later Euclid, associated the four polyhedrons with the four classical elements (left to right on the patch): tetrahedron, fire; cube, earth; octahedron, air; icosahedron, water. The fifth solid is the dodecahedron, represented by the three-dimensional shape of the patch, which the Greeks associated with aether, the celestial energy that fills the universe, represented here by the cosmic background. Fire stood for the studies of combustion science undertaken during the mission; earth for crystallography; and air and water for the fluid-physics research. The mathematical symbol for infinity is also included, and this stands for the fluid-mechanics investigations. In the centre, we see Columbia travelling through space with the initials of the United States Microgravity Laboratory (USML) beneath it. The final artwork was produced by graphic artist David Russell with creative guidance from mission pilot Kent Rominger.

During the 16-day flight, the crew was split into two teams so work could be continued around the clock within the Spacelab facility.

Left to right: (back) Cady Coleman, Kenneth Bowersox, Fred Leslie, Kathryn Thornton; (front) Albert Sacco, Kent Rominger, Michael López-Alegría

CREW

Kenneth D. Cameron – Commander
James D. Halsell Jr – Pilot
Chris A. Hadfield – Mission Specialist (CSA)
Jerry L. Ross – Mission Specialist
William S. McArthur Jr – Mission Specialist

SPACECRAFT

Atlantis, OV-104

LAUNCH DATE

12 November 1995

MISSION

• Second docking with Russian Mir space station.
• Delivery of the Shuttle–Mir docking module.

Left to right: (back) William McArthur, Jerry Ross,
Chris Hadfield; (front) James Halsell, Kenneth Cameron

The bright blazing sunrise announces a new era of human presence in space, that of the space station. Designed with the crew members' creative input, the STS-74 patch shows the cabin and forward section of the shuttle's payload bay while docked with Mir. The Russian-built docking module inside the payload bay is illustrated with a shading effect to symbolize its pivotal role in bringing the USA and Russia together on this second docking of the joint Shuttle–Mir programme. The module was delivered to the space station as a permanent extension so that future dockings would be more efficient. Earth's horizon features in the background, the layers of its atmosphere indicated by a colourful spectrum. The flags of the three nations involved in this mission are illustrated at the bottom: the USA, Canada and Russia.

The primary objective of STS-74 was to deliver supplies and equipment to Mir. As well as the new docking module, the crew of Atlantis brought two solar arrays and gifts for their cosmonaut friends, including Canadian maple-syrup sweets and a guitar.

DID YOU KNOW?

Chris Hadfield of the Canadian Space Agency was the fourth Canadian in space and the first Canadian shuttle mission specialist.

CREW

Brian Duffy – Commander
Brent W. Jett Jr – Pilot
Leroy Chiao – Mission Specialist
Winston E. Scott – Mission Specialist
Koichi Wakata – Mission Specialist (NASDA)
Daniel T. Barry – Mission Specialist

SPACECRAFT

Endeavour, OV-105

LAUNCH DATE

11 January 1996

MISSION

- Retrieval of the Japanese microgravity research spacecraft, Space Flyer Unit (SFU).
- Deployment and retrieval of the Office of Aeronautics and Space Technology-Flyer (OAST-Flyer)

The primary objectives of this nine-day mission are neatly captured in the patch design. The small, yellow spacecraft with the solar array panels is the Japanese Space Flyer Unit (SFU). This had been launched from Japan in March 1995 and had been gathering vital data on microgravity experiments, technology development and astronomical observations. The crew of STS-72 were tasked with retrieving the SFU to return it to Earth for analysis. The square, yellow payload being deployed by Endeavour's robotic arm is the Office of Aeronautics and Space Technology-Flyer (OAST-Flyer). For two days, the OAST-Flyer flew at a distance of 45 miles (72 kilometres) from the orbiter, collecting data from a series of on-board microgravity experiments. Also illustrated inside the payload bay is equipment for the Shuttle Laser Altimeter (SLA) and the Shuttle Solar Backscatter Ultraviolet Instrument (SSBUI). The astronaut symbolizes two scheduled EVAs which lasted 13 hours in total, testing an array of techniques to prepare for the construction of the International Space Station. One unique design feature is that the mission patch is clearly visible on the astronaut's left shoulder. The artwork – created by NASA artist Sean Collins with creative guidance from astronaut Daniel Barry – incorporates many hidden references personal to the crew including a basketball in the payload bay and initials of the astronaut's children on the OAST-Flyer and inside the payload bay. A very keen eye will notice an upside-down cat's head and a pig on the astronaut's helmet, in reference to astronaut selection group 13 (The Hairballs) and group 14 (The Hogs). The tiny yellow stars over the USA and Japan pinpoint the various home towns of the crew.

Left to right: (back) Winston Scott, Leroy Chiao, Koichi Wakata, Daniel Barry; (front) Brent Jett, Brian Duffy

CREW

Andrew M. Allen – Commander
Scott J. 'Doc' Horowitz – Pilot
Franklin R. Chang-Díaz – Payload Commander
Jeffrey A. Hoffman – Mission Specialist
Maurizio Cheli – Mission Specialist (ESA)
Claude Nicollier – Mission Specialist (ESA)
Umberto Guidoni – Payload Specialist (ASI)

SPACECRAFT

Columbia, OV-102

LAUNCH DATE

22 February 1996

MISSION

- Tethered Satellite System (TSS-1R).
- Spacelab mission. United States Microgravity Payload-3.

Left to right: (back) Maurizio Cheli, Umberto Guidoni, Jeffrey Hoffman, Claude Nicollier; (front) Doc Horowitz, Andrew Allen, Franklin Chang-Díaz

Designed by artist Mike Sanni, the STS-75 mission patch features the joint US/Italian Tethered Satellite System (TSS-1R) attached to Columbia on its 12-mile (19-kilometre) tether. The United States Microgravity Payload (USMP-3) was also on board (for the third time) in order to conduct studies in materials science and thermodynamics. The mission patch depicts TSS-1R's tether stretching across the terminator – the line that divides day and night on Earth. This is to mark the dawn of a new era in tethered operations to study Earth's atmosphere. The TSS-1R observed the electrodynamic activity of a tether system in the ionosphere, the electrically charged layer of Earth's upper atmosphere. The TSS-1R and Columbia are seen flying through Earth's geomagnetic field – suggested by the fine blue lines on the right of the patch – which produces thousands of volts of electricity. The crew's names are listed down the left-hand side of the insignia.

The mission lasted nearly 16 days and completed 252 revolutions of Earth.

DID YOU KNOW?

The Tethered Satellite System (TSS) had already flown on STS-46, but the experiment had been cut short following a jammed tether. On STS-75, the satellite was relaying valuable data when suddenly the tether snapped, and the TSS drifted away.

CREW

Kevin P. Chilton – Commander
Richard A. Searfoss – Pilot
Ronald M. Sega – Mission Specialist
Michael R. 'Rich' Clifford – Mission Specialist
Linda M. Godwin – Mission Specialist
Shannon W. Lucid – Mir 'up' crew

SPACECRAFT

Atlantis, OV-104

LAUNCH DATE

22 March 1996

MISSION

• Third docking to Russian Mir space station.
• SPACEHAB single module on board.

The STS-76 mission-patch artwork pays homage to the 'Spirit of 76' of the American Revolution. The number 76 is surrounded by the 13 stars of the 'Betsy Ross' flag, an early incarnation of the Stars and Stripes. The artwork sees Atlantis manoeuvring to rendezvous and dock with Mir, surrounded by six stars representing the shuttle crew and two small planets for the Russian crew already on board the space station. The gold trail of Atlantis recalls the astronaut badge and America's vital role in human space exploration. The two astronauts in the border mark the first US EVA of the Shuttle–Mir programme, during which experiments were attached to the space station and procedures tested for future spacewalks on the International Space Station. The patch was conceived by the crew members and astronaut Michael R. 'Rich' Clifford's 12-year-old son Brandon. Artist Sean Collins completed the final artwork.

Norman Thagard had previously spent almost four months on Mir after arriving there on board a Russian Soyuz capsule, but STS-76 saw the start of US and Russian crew members being transferred to and from the space station via the shuttle.

DID YOU KNOW?
NASA's Shannon Lucid transferred to Mir and stayed alongside the Russian crew for a total of 179 days. She was the first shuttle crew member to do so and the first American woman to live on a space station.

Left to right: (back) Michael Clifford, Shannon Lucid, Linda Godwin; (front) Ronald Sega, Kevin Chilton, Richard Searfoss

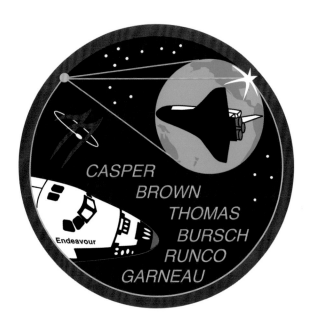

CREW

John H. Casper – Commander
Curtis L. Brown Jr – Pilot
Andrew S. Thomas – Mission Specialist
Daniel W. Bursch – Mission Specialist
Mario Runco Jr – Mission Specialist
Marc Garneau – Mission Specialist (CSA)

SPACECRAFT

Endeavour, OV-105

LAUNCH DATE

19 May 1996

MISSION

• SPACEHAB-4 mission.
• Deployment and retrieval of SPARTAN (IAE).

Left to right: (back) Daniel Bursch, Mario Runco,
Marc Garneau, Andrew Thomas; (front) Curtis Brown,
John Casper

STS-77 carried two primary payloads: the SPACEHAB-4 scientific facility and the Shuttle Pointed Autonomous Research Tool for Astronomy (SPARTAN) Inflatable Antenna Experiment (IAE). The small gold circle on the mission patch (top left) is the SPARTAN, and the three gold lines protruding from it are the struts attached to its circular concave parabolic mirror (here replaced by Earth). The shuttle is reflected within the 'mirror' as are the shuttle's rendezvous operations with the Passive Aerodynamically Stabilized Magnetically Damped Satellite – Satellite Test Unit (PAMS-STU), part of Technology Experiments for Advancing Missions in Space (TEAMS). The PAMS-STU satellite reflects the Sun on the horizon (top right) and is positioned over the Goddard Space Flight Center, Maryland, where the SPARTAN/IAE and TEAMS experiments were developed. We see North America (for the home nations of the US/Canadian crew) and the Pacific Ocean, which recalls the voyages of HMS Endeavour, Captain James Cook's ship. Ursa Minor can be seen at the top of the patch, the 11 stars of which celebrate the 11th flight of Endeavour as well as the 11 TEAMS experiments that would be undertaken.

The four stars of the Southern Cross on the right mark the fourth flight of SPACEHAB. SPARTAN's central gold strut, along with the gold inner line of the border, represent the shape of SPACEHAB in cross-section. The red 77 and orbiting satellite is an adaptation of the NASA logo that tells us the mission number.

CREW

Terence T. 'Tom' Henricks – Commander
Kevin R. Kregel – Pilot
Richard M. Linnehan – Mission Specialist
Susan J. Helms – Mission Specialist
Charles E. Brady Jr – Mission Specialist
Jean-Jacques Favier – Payload Specialist (CNES)
Robert Brent Thirsk – Payload Specialist (CSA)

SPACECRAFT

Columbia, OV-102

LAUNCH DATE

20 June 1996

MISSION

• Life and Microgravity Spacelab mission.

STS-78 was an international mission involving scientists from ten countries and the collaboration of five space agencies: NASA plus the European, French, Canadian and Italian organizations. The patch, which is influenced stylistically by Northwest Native American art, illustrates Columbia invoking the spirit of an eagle in the form of a totem pole, so linking America's past with its present. The eagle was seen as a sign of strength and power among Native Americans and is a national emblem of the USA. The shuttle's wings are stylized as eagle feathers, a Native American symbol of peace and friendship. The totem-art LMS on the payload-bay doors is for the Life and Microgravity Spacelab (LMS) facility carried by Columbia. The Sun, a Native American symbol of life, holds three icons resembling crystals, which relate to the three high-temperature microgravity materials-processing facilities on board. The nine stars to the right represent the seven crew members plus the two backup payload specialists, Pedro Duque and Luca Urbani, who worked alongside them during preparations. The constellation Delphinus, the Dolphin, is top right; dolphins were often considered friends to ancient mariners and have been reported to guide sailors to safety. This distinctive patch was designed by Tsimshian/Norwegian artist William 'Bill' Helin.

The patch also pays tribute to the 1996 Olympic Games in Atlanta, Georgia. Three coloured circles of the Olympic rings can be seen on the shuttle's engines. They are positioned over Atlanta, thus marking the location of this extra show of unity among nations. Earth's limb and four upper atmospheric layers resemble a rainbow, also a sign of peace.

Left to right: (back) Jean-Jacques Favier, Richard Linnehan, Susan Helms, Charles Brady, Robert Brent Thirsk; (front) Tom Henricks, Kevin Kregel

CREW

William F. Readdy – Commander
Terrence W. Wilcutt – Pilot
Jerome 'Jay' Apt – Mission Specialist
Thomas D. Akers – Mission Specialist
Carl E. Walz – Mission Specialist
John E. Blaha – Mir 'up' crew
Shannon W. Lucid – Mir 'down' crew

SPACECRAFT

Atlantis, OV-104

LAUNCH DATE

16 September 1996

MISSION

• Fourth docking to the Russian Mir space station.

Left to right: (back) Shannon Lucid, John Blaha;
(front) Jay Apt, Terrence Wilcutt, William Readdy,
Thomas Akers, Carl Walz

The continued joint operations between the USA and Russia on this fourth docking with Mir is the theme of this patch. Its shape resembles that of the airlock hatch of Atlantis, backdropped by the national flags of the two nations so opening a gateway to friendship and cooperation in space between NASA and the Russian Space Agency. The handshake between astronaut and cosmonaut during an EVA highlights the unity and teamwork of the mission as well as the work of both nations' space agencies and scientists back on Earth. At the bottom we see the words Shuttle–Mir, with Mir written in Cyrillic letters. The top arch of the patch displays the names of the core five crew members, while the bottom left and right sections feature the NASA astronauts who will be transferred to and relieved from Mir. Shannon Lucid's name is shown reading downwards as she is returning home after 188 days in space, of which 179 were on board Mir; John Blaha's name reads upwards, telling us that he will journey up to the station to begin his stay.

As well as delivering new supplies and equipment to Mir, the mission also featured the first flight of the SPACEHAB Double Module configuration inside the payload bay of Atlantis, carrying an array of experiments for the crew to undertake. Mir also transferred completed experiment samples and equipment onto the shuttle for delivery back to Earth.

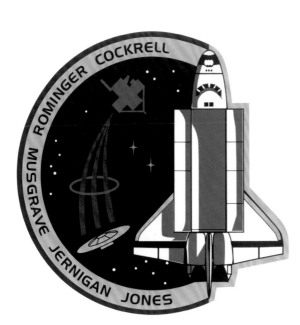

CREW

Kenneth D. Cockrell – Commander
Kent V. Rominger – Pilot
F. Story Musgrave – Mission Specialist
Thomas D. Jones – Mission Specialist
Tamara E. Jernigan – Mission Specialist

SPACECRAFT

Columbia, OV-102

LAUNCH DATE

19 November 1996

MISSION

• Deployment and retrieval of ORFEUS-SPAS II and WSF-3.

The STS-80 artwork has Columbia set against the border of the patch with its payload-bay doors open. The scene to the shuttle's left features the Orbiting Retrievable Far and Extreme Ultraviolet Spectrograph-Shuttle Pallet Satellite (ORFEUS-SPAS) being deployed at the top of the patch and the Wake Shield Facility (WSF) free-flyer satellite being deployed at the bottom. The three red lines converging with a blue ring surrounding them resemble the astronaut badge, once again emphasizing the importance of human space exploration for scientific advancement and research into new technology. There are 16 stars arranged in various constellations, one star for each day of the planned mission duration and in honour of the stellar teams on the ground. The two blue stars represent the two planned EVAs that were to take place on the mission.

The ORFEUS-SPAS II was designed to study the evolution of stars and galaxies. The WSF free-flying disc was designed to grow ultra-purity semiconductors in microgravity for use in advanced electronics. The two planned EVAs were both cancelled because of a problem with the shuttle's airlock hatch.

DID YOU KNOW?

At a total of 17 days, 15 hours and 53 minutes, STS-80 was the longest mission of the Space Shuttle Program.

Left to right: Kent Rominger, Tamara Jernigan, Story Musgrave, Thomas Jones, Kenneth Cockrell

CREW

Michael A. Baker – Commander
Brent W. Jett Jr – Pilot
Peter J. K. 'Jeff' Wisoff – Mission Specialist
John M. Grunsfeld – Mission Specialist
Marsha S. Ivins – Mission Specialist
Jerry M. Linenger – Mir 'up' crew
John E. Blaha – Mir 'down' crew

SPACECRAFT

Atlantis, OV-104

LAUNCH DATE

12 January 1997

MISSION

• Fifth docking to the Russian Mir space station.

Left to right: (back) John Grunsfeld, John Blaha, Jeff Wisoff, Jerry Linenger, Marsha Ivins; (front) Brent Jett, Michael Baker

This mission patch artwork was designed to resemble the Roman numeral V (5) to mark this being the fifth docking of the Shuttle–Mir programme. Atlantis is illustrated launching into the sky to begin its ten-day mission orbiting Earth, and Mir can be seen silhouetted in the background. The crew spent five days docked with the space station, and American astronaut Jerry Linenger replaced John Blaha as part of the Mir crew. The flags of the USA and Russia are a strong feature of the design, symbolizing the collaboration of the two nations on these successful Shuttle–Mir operations that were designed to increase the understanding of how humans can live in space. The crew collaborated with graphic artist Sean Collins to produce this original insignia.

After being with the Russians for 118 days, John Blaha returned home with the STS-81 crew, completing his final mission in space. During the time Atlantis was docked with Mir, the crews transferred new supplies, scientific equipment and logistics to the station, and the shuttle was loaded with an extensive array of experiments conducted on Mir. Atlantis once again carried the SPACEHAB double module inside its payload bay during the mission.

CREW

Kenneth D. Bowersox – Commander
Scott J. 'Doc' Horowitz – Pilot
Mark C. Lee – Payload Commander
Joseph R. Tanner – Mission Specialist
Steven A. Hawley – Mission Specialist
Gregory J. Harbaugh – Mission Specialist
Steven L. Smith – Mission Specialist

SPACECRAFT

Discovery, OV-103

LAUNCH DATE

11 February 1997

MISSION

• Second Hubble Space Telescope servicing mission.

STS-82 was a mission to service the Hubble Space Telescope (HST), and Hubble is the dominant element of this patch. HST is NASA's flagship space observatory, studying the far reaches of the universe and capturing images of distant stars, galaxies and nebulae as well as accruing knowledge about our solar system. In the artwork, Hubble is shown as it would appear as the crew of Discovery manoeuvre to rendezvous with it, looking out towards the stars with its solar array panels extended. The spiral galaxy illustrated at the top represents Hubble's objective to accurately determine the cosmic-distance scale. The yellow celestial object surrounded by four blue objects stands for a discovery made by Hubble, known as a gravitational lens, which is a cluster of celestial objects (such as stars or galaxies) that is between the viewer and another distant light source in the universe. The crew members who participated in EVA repairs to the telescope are named at the top of the patch, with the prime shuttle crew at the bottom.

The shuttle's Remote Manipulator System robotic arm was used to capture HST and place it in the payload bay. During the ten-day mission, five spacewalks were conducted to carry out servicing duties on HST. Astronauts Lee and Smith alternated with Tanner and Harbaugh for EVA duties that lasted more than 33 hours in total.

Left to right: (back) Joseph Tanner, Gregory Harbaugh, Mark Lee, Steven Smith; (front) Kenneth Bowersox, Steven Hawley, Doc Horowitz

STS-83

CREW

James D. Halsell Jr – Commander
Susan L. Still – Pilot
Janice E. Voss – Payload Commander
Michael L. Gernhardt – Mission Specialist
Donald A. Thomas – Mission Specialist
Roger K. Crouch – Payload Specialist
Greg T. Linteris – Payload Specialist

SPACECRAFT

Columbia, OV-102

LAUNCH DATE

4 April 1997

MISSION

• First flight of the Microgravity Science Laboratory-1.

STS-83 marked the first flight of the Microgravity Science Laboratory-1, a facility to study the scientific fields of combustion science, fluid dynamics, biotechnology and materials processing. The mission would also test new hardware, facilities and procedures to be used on future missions on the International Space Station. The mission patch artwork – designed by artist Mark Pestana – features Columbia soaring into space leaving a red 'S' trail behind to state the scientific objectives of the mission. The eclipse in the centre represents Earth as well as a liquid droplet in microgravity, a nod to the fluid-dynamics and materials-science experiments on the mission. The combustion experiments are there in the blue starburst burning in space.

STS-83 mission was cut short during the fourth day, as there were concerns about one of the shuttle's three fuel cells. The entire crew were given the opportunity to refly the mission three months later on STS-94.

DID YOU KNOW?
The shuttle's three fuel cells were used to produce electricity and provide drinking water for the mission. Even though one is sufficient, NASA rules state that all three must be working to ensure the crew's safe return.

Left to right: (back) Roger Crouch, Greg Linteris, Michael Gernhardt; (front) Janice Voss, James Halsell, Susan Still, Donald Thomas

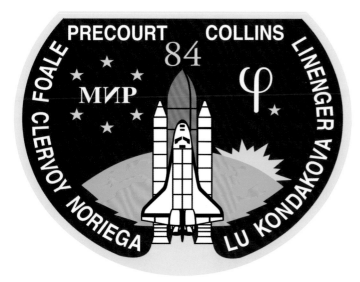

CREW

Charles J. Precourt – Commander
Eileen M. Collins – Pilot
Jean-François Clervoy – Mission Specialist (ESA)
Carlos I. Noriega – Mission Specialist
Edward T. Lu – Mission Specialist
Yelena V. Kondakova – Mission Specialist (RKA)
C. Michael Foale – Mir 'up' crew
Jerry M. Linenger – Mir 'down' crew

SPACECRAFT

Atlantis, OV-104

LAUNCH DATE

15 May 1997

MISSION

• Sixth docking to the Russian Mir space station.

STS-84 was the sixth docking mission in the Shuttle–Mir programme and Phase One of the International Space Station programme. The mission patch depicts Atlantis at lift-off on its way to deliver supplies and logistics to Mir. The Phase One programme, the opening of a new chapter of the human presence in space, is represented by the rising sun as well as the Greek letter phi and one star. To the left of Atlantis, Mir is written in Cyrillic characters and surrounded by six stars for the sixth docking. The seven stars on the patch are the six Mir modules taken into orbit by Russian spacecraft plus the single module delivered by Atlantis on an earlier mission, the seven modules of which Mir was comprised. The names of the commander and pilot are featured at the top and the four mission specialists are shown at the bottom. Michael Foale replaced Jerry Linenger as part of the Mir crew, and his name is written facing upwards, while Linenger is written facing downwards to signpost this transfer. The patch is designed in the shape of the cross-section of the SPACEHAB double module that was located inside the shuttle's payload bay.

Michael Foale was tasked with completing a number of investigations during his stay on Mir. These included experiments in advanced technology, biological studies, human life sciences, crystal growth, space-station risk mitigation, materials processing, microgravity sciences and Earth observations.

Left to right: (back) Jean-François Clervoy, Eileen Collins, Edward Lu, Yelena Kondakova, Carlos Noriega; (front) Jerry Linenger, Charles Precourt, Michael Foale

CREW

James D. Halsell Jr – Commander
Susan L. Still – Pilot
Janice E. Voss – Payload Commander
Michael L. Gernhardt – Mission Specialist
Donald A. Thomas – Mission Specialist
Roger K. Crouch – Payload Specialist
Greg T. Linteris – Payload Specialist

SPACECRAFT

Columbia, OV-102

LAUNCH DATE

July 1997

MISSION

Reflight of the Microgravity Science Laboratory-1
mission.

Left to right: (back) Donald Thomas, Roger Crouch;
(middle) Michael Gernhardt, James Halsell, Greg Linteris;
(front) Susan Still, Janice Voss

The mission patch for STS-94 is a colour variation of the STS-83 mission
patch, both created by artist Mark Pestana. Here the blues – and the red
of the S trail and MSL – are lighter than before, and the border is the same
colour as the centre rather than red, as in the patch for the previous mission.

STS-83 had been cut short after just four days in space because of fuel-cell
problems, and the astronauts launched again on STS-94 to carry out the
objectives of the original mission (see page 134). The crew was split into
two teams to allow for 24-hour investigations into various scientific fields,
including protein crystal growth, to help scientists research and investigate
treatments for diseases such as cancer, diabetes and HIV.

DID YOU KNOW?

*STS-94 was the first time NASA launched a reflight with the same crew,
the same payload and in the same orbiter.*

STS-85

CREW

Curtis L. Brown Jr – Commander
Kent V. Rominger – Pilot
Nancy J. Davis – Mission Specialist
Robert L. Curbeam Jr – Mission Specialist
Stephen K. Robinson – Mission Specialist
Bjarni V. Tryggvason – Payload Specialist (CSA)

SPACECRAFT

Discovery, OV-103

LAUNCH DATE

7 August 1997

MISSION

• Deployment and retrieval of CRISTA-SPAS-02, IEH-02, TAS-01.

Here we see Discovery in orbit with its bay doors wide open, exposing the various payloads within. At the front is the Manipulator Flight Demonstration robotic arm, which was used as a test for the Japanese robotic arm later installed on the International Space Station. The International Extreme Ultraviolet Hitchhiker, visible at the back of the payload bay, was used to study celestial objects – symbolized by the three stars (top right) – and solar extreme ultraviolet energy in space, specifically that from Jupiter, which is the orange planet to the right of the shuttle's nose. The comet Hale-Bopp, which was visible from Earth at the time of the mission, is featured in the middle of the cluster of stars. The Technology Applications and Science experiment is also to be found in the middle of Discovery's payload bay. The arrowhead-shaped object to the right is the Cryogenic Infrared Spectrometers and Telescopes for the Atmosphere-Shuttle Pallet Satellite-2 (CRISTA-SPAS-02), the purpose of which was to collect data on the chemical composition of Earth's atmosphere. The yellow trajectory marks the shuttle's high-inclination orbit over northern latitudes. The blazing sun to the left is for the daytime operations performed over the northern hemisphere and the solar experiments conducted throughout the mission.

STS-85 lasted nearly 12 full days, completing 185 revolutions of Earth and travelling a total orbital distance of 4.7 million miles (7.6 million kilometres).

Left to right: (back) Robert Curbeam, Stephen Robinson, Nancy Davis, Bjarni Tryggvason; (front): Curtis Brown, Kent Rominger

STS-86

CREW

James D. Wetherbee – Commander
Michael J. Bloomfield – Pilot
Vladimir G. Titov – Mission Specialist (RKA)
Scott E. Parazynski – Mission Specialist
Jean-Loup Chrétien – Mission Specialist (CNES)
Wendy B. Lawrence – Mission Specialist
David A. Wolf – Mir 'up' crew
C. Michael Foale – Mir 'down' crew

SPACECRAFT

Atlantis, OV-104

LAUNCH DATE

25 September 1997

MISSION

• Seventh docking to the Russian Mir space station.

STS-86 was the seventh docking in the Shuttle–Mir programme, and central to artist Mark Pestana's design is a Mercator projection of Earth, which reiterates the international collaborative nature of the flight. Once again we have the astronaut emblem, this time formed by the red, white and blue rays that project up towards the yellow star. The rays' lower section recalls the US flag – with seven stars marking the seventh Shuttle–Mir docking – while the upper section leading to the star is the Russian flag. The yellow and white orbital trajectories of the shuttle and space station shoot across the front of the patch as they prepare to rendezvous and dock. The astronaut and cosmonaut seen either side of the patch refer to the joint spacewalk conducted on the mission.

David Wolf was transferred to Mir to begin his stay on the space station, replacing Michael Foale after a total of 145 days in space, 134 of which were spent living and working on Mir.

DID YOU KNOW?
During the six days that Atlantis was docked with Mir during STS-86, more than four tons of material from the SPACEHAB Double Module was transferred over, including water, experiment hardware, batteries and three air-pressurization units, plus a vast amount of logistics.

Left to right: (back) Jean-Loup Chrétien, Scott Parazynski, Vladimir Titov, Michael Foale; (front) David Wolf, Michael Bloomfield, James Wetherbee, Wendy Lawrence

CREW

Kevin R. Kregel – Commander
Steven W. Lindsey – Pilot
Kalpana Chawla – Mission Specialist
Winston E. Scott – Mission Specialist
Takao Doi – Mission Specialist (NASDA)
Leonid Kadenyuk – Payload Specialist (NSAU)

SPACECRAFT

Columbia, OV-102

LAUNCH DATE

19 November 1997

MISSION

- United States Microgravity Payload-4 (USMP-4).
- Deployment and retrieval of SPARTAN-201-04.

In something of a departure in design, this patch is shaped like a space helmet because STS-87's mission would include an EVA to test tools and techniques that would be required for the assembly of the International Space Station. Earth forms the back of the helmet, while the visor is the border, the Sun's corona and deep space in the background. Columbia bisects the two sections thereby linking Earth with the cosmos. The three red lines emanating from the shuttle's payload bay recall the astronaut badge as well as standing in for the shuttle's Remote Manipulator System robotic arm, which was to deploy and retrieve the SPARTAN-201-04, a satellite designed to study the Sun's corona, hence the orange flames. The microgravity µg symbol is there for the scientific experiments on this United States Microgravity Payload-4 mission. The outer border of the visor displays the names of all six astronauts, including Leonid Kadenyuk, the first Ukrainian to fly on the shuttle; the Ukrainian national flag sits beside his name. Artist David Russell created the artwork with mission specialist Kalpana Chawla.

The SPARTAN-201-04 was deployed from the payload bay, but the satellite failed to obtain the desired altitude. Capture of the SPARTAN using the shuttle's robotic arm was unsuccessful, so astronauts Winston Scott and Takao Doi conducted an EVA to retrieve it.

DID YOU KNOW?

Takao Doi was the first Japanese astronaut to perform a spacewalk.

Left to right: (back) Winston Scott, Takao Doi; (middle) Kalpana Chawla, Leonid Kadenyuk; (front) Steven Lindsey, Kevin Kregel

STS-89

CREW

Terrence W. Wilcutt – Commander
Joe F. Edwards Jr – Pilot
James F. Reilly II – Mission Specialist
Michael P. Anderson – Mission Specialist
Bonnie J. Dunbar – Mission Specialist
Salizhan Sharipov – Mission Specialist (RKA)
Andrew S. W. Thomas – Mir 'up' crew
David A. Wolf – Mir 'down' crew

SPACECRAFT

Endeavour, OV-105

LAUNCH DATE

22 January 1998

MISSION

• Eighth docking with the Russian Mir space station.

Left to right: (back) David Wolf, Salizhan Sharipov,
James Reilly, Andrew Thomas, Michael Anderson;
(front) Joe F. Edwards, Terrence Wilcutt, Bonnie Dunbar

STS-89 was the eighth docking in the Shuttle–Mir programme, and the mission-patch artwork – once again by Mark Pestana – shows Endeavour and Mir over the Bering Strait separating Russia and Alaska. As the space-station era gets under way, a silhouetted International Space Station (ISS) can be seen in the background with the Sun shining brightly behind it. In the foreground, Mir and Endeavour are lit up by the blazing sunrise in acknowledgement of the Shuttle–Mir programme's vital role in the development of the ISS. The nine stars are the nine Shuttle–Mir docking missions but also stand for the children of the crew, whose generation will benefit from the USA and Russia working together to further human scientific knowledge and continue the exploration of our planet and the universe. The inner border of the patch forms the number eight – the eighth docking with Mir – and together with the nine stars represents the mission number: 89. The colours of the border are the red, white and blue of both nations' flags, which also appear either side of the patch.

The crew members' names are shown around the border, with Russian mission specialist Salizhan Sharipov in Cyrillic characters. Andrew Thomas was transferred to Mir on arrival, and his name is written pointing upwards; David Wolf joined the crew of Endeavour after spending 199 days living on the space station, and his name is written downwards to show that he is on his way home.

STS-90

CREW

Richard A. Searfoss – Commander
Scott D. Altman – Pilot
Dafydd R. 'Dave' Williams – Mission Specialist (CSA)
Kathryn P. 'Kay' Hire – Mission Specialist
Richard M. Linnehan – Mission Specialist
Jay C. Buckey Jr – Payload Specialist
James A. Pawelczyk – Payload Specialist

SPACECRAFT

Columbia, OV-102

LAUNCH DATE

17 April 1998

MISSION

• Final Spacelab mission.

Neuroscience and gaining a greater understanding of the structure and functionality of the human brain formed the main thrust of STS-90. The 26 experiments of the on board Neurolab dealt with studies of the nervous system in microgravity, as part of the USA's 'Decade of the Brain' initiative. Columbia is featured orbiting Earth, which can be seen through a neuron-shaped window. Spacelab, which was built by the European Space Agency, can be seen within the shuttle's payload bay, a reminder of the international nature of this significant research mission. The nine stars are for the seven crew members plus the two backup payload specialists, Alexander W. Dunlap and Chiaki Mukai. They form the constellation Cetus, the Whale, as a reference to the United Nations having declared 1998 International Year of the Ocean. The Moon and Mars are present as future destinations, while the distant stars acknowledge the various space agencies and teams around the world who have contributed to the International Space Station and the role it will have in advancing human knowledge.

This internationally sponsored mission spent 16 days in orbit conducting life-science research. Crew members participated in experiments as well as other test subjects, including rats, mice, crickets, snails and fish.

DID YOU KNOW?
STS-90 was the final flight of the Spacelab science module.

Left to right: (back) James Pawelczyk, Richard Linnehan, Kay Hire, Dave Williams, Jay Buckey; (front) Scott Altman, Richard Searfoss

141

CREW

Charles J. Precourt – Commander
Dominic L. Pudwill Gorie – Pilot
Franklin R. Chang-Díaz – Mission Specialist
Wendy B. Lawrence – Mission Specialist
Janet L. Kavandi – Mission Specialist
Valery Ryumin – Mission Specialist (RKA)
Andrew S. W. Thomas – Mir 'down' crew

SPACECRAFT

Discovery, OV-103

LAUNCH DATE

2 June 1998

MISSION

• Ninth and final docking with the Russian Mir space station.

Left to right: (back) Franklin Chang-Díaz, Janet Kavandi, Valery Ryumin; (middle) Wendy Lawrence, Andrew Thomas; (front) Dominic Gorie, Charles Precourt

The STS-91 mission patch pays tribute to the ninth and final docking with Mir. The flight marked the last stage of Phase One in the Shuttle–Mir programme and paved the way for the construction of the International Space Station in Phase Two. The design sees Discovery approaching Mir high above Earth with the USA and Russia directly below in recognition of the joint efforts of both nations on these revolutionary spaceflights. The Alpha Magnetic Spectrometer (AMS) flew in space for the first time and is visible inside the shuttle's payload bay. Two gold streaks, representing charged elementary particles, can be seen entering the AMS. The objectives of the AMS were to discover dark and missing matter to help scientists gain a greater understanding of the origins of the universe. Andrew Thomas returned home with the shuttle crew after spending 130 days on Mir. The crew members' names are displayed around the edge of the patch, with Russian mission specialist Valery Ryumin's in Cyrillic characters. The mission number and flags of both nations are featured at the top of the design.

The mission marked the end of 907 continuous days in space by alternating American and Russian crews. As well as delivering new supplies, experiments, logistics and water to the space station, long-term US experiments were transferred from Mir to Discovery for analysis back on Earth. The shuttle crew also conducted experiments during the flight, including in the fields of biomedical science, combustion science and crystal growth.

CREW

Curtis L. Brown Jr – Commander
Steven W. Lindsey – Pilot
Pedro Duque – Mission Specialist (ESA)
Scott E. Parazynski – Mission Specialist
Stephen K. Robinson – Mission Specialist
Chiaki Mukai – Payload Specialist (NASDA)
John H. Glenn Jr – Payload Specialist

SPACECRAFT

Discovery, OV-103

LAUNCH DATE

29 October 1998

MISSION

- Mercury astronaut and US Senator John Glenn returns to space.

STS-95 witnessed the return to space of America's first orbital astronaut, John Glenn, and the artwork links the scientific objectives of the mission with the historical significance of Glenn's presence. Discovery is seen rising up towards Earth's limb, highlighting the benefits humankind will gain from the shuttle's scientific studies as well as those on the SPARTAN-201-05 solar observatory that was released and retrieved by the shuttle. The coloured rocket plumes represent the three main fields of science to be studied on the mission: microgravity material science, medical research and astronomy. The red plume extends up over the shuttle to form the number 7: for the seven crew members of Discovery, to celebrate Glenn's 1962 Friendship 7 flight and to honour all the Mercury 7 astronauts. Glenn's historic flight is remembered by the small red Mercury capsule orbiting the shuttle at the centre of the patch.

The shuttle carried the SPACEHAB pressurized module in its payload bay, and more than 80 scientific experiments were conducted during the flight.

DID YOU KNOW?

John Glenn was the first American to orbit Earth in 1962 on Mercury-Atlas 6, the third human spaceflight by the USA. He completed three Earth orbits in his Friendship 7 spacecraft. Although Glenn was the first American in orbit, the USSR's Yuri Gagarin had already orbited Earth in Vostok 1, followed by Gherman Titov in Vostok 2.

Left to right: (back) Scott Parazynski, Stephen Robinson, Pedro Duque, John Glenn; (middle) Chiaki Mukai; (front) Steven Lindsey, Curtis Brown

CREW

Robert D. Cabana – Commander
Frederick W. Sturckow – Pilot
Jerry L. Ross – Mission Specialist
Nancy J. Currie (née Sherlock) – Mission Specialist
James H. Newman – Mission Specialist
Sergei K. Krikalev – Mission Specialist (RKA)

SPACECRAFT

Endeavour, OV-105

LAUNCH DATE

4 December 1998

MISSION

First International Space Station Assembly Mission 2A.
Delivery of first US module (Unity Node 1).

Left to right: (back) Jerry Ross, Robert Cabana,
Frederick Sturckow, James Newman; (front) Sergei Krikalev,
Nancy Currie

In order to start in-orbit construction work on the International Space Station (ISS), the crew of STS-88 delivered the Unity module into orbit and manually attached it during EVAs to the Russian-made Zarya module that had arrived in orbit two weeks earlier on an unpiloted Russian rocket. The patch design shows Unity inside the shuttle's payload bay as the crew captures the Zarya module with the Remote Manipulator System robotic arm. The Russian name Zarya translates as 'sunrise', signifying this new era of international cooperation, and the patch highlights this with the rising Sun on the right. The Earth below shows the countries that contributed to this effort: the USA, Russia, Europe (ESA), Japan and Canada. The Big Dipper, or the Plough, is also shown. This constellation has been used by generations of explorers to locate the North Star, seen to the right of Zarya; here it stands for the international efforts of everyone involved in the development of the ISS to guide humankind into a new phase of space exploration. Artist Sean Collins created the artwork with creative direction from the crew of Endeavour.

All mission objectives were completed, and the two connected modules were powered up. Secondary mission objectives were the deployment of the shuttle's KU-band antenna and a Hitchhiker payload consisting of a number of small satellites.

DID YOU KNOW?
STS-88 was the first shuttle flight to the International Space Station (ISS).

ROMINGER HUSBAND
PAYETTE TOKAPEB
JERNIGAN OCHOA BARRY

STS-96

CREW

Kent V. Rominger – Commander
Rick D. Husband – Pilot
Daniel T. Barry – Mission Specialist
Ellen Ochoa – Mission Specialist
Tamara E. Jernigan – Mission Specialist
Julie Payette – Mission Specialist (CSA)
Valeri I. Tokarev – Mission Specialist (RKA)

SPACECRAFT

Discovery, OV-103

LAUNCH DATE

27 May 1999

MISSION

- International Space Station Assembly Mission 2A.1.
- First docking to the International Space Station.

The STS-96 insignia commemorates the first shuttle to dock with the International Space Station (ISS) and the second assembly mission. It focuses on the themes of the ISS programme: Earth research, human space exploration and international cooperation. The combined modules Zarya and Unity are illustrated orbiting Earth while Discovery prepares for the first docking. The three vertical lines pointing towards the star and the yellow orbital trajectory of Discovery recall the astronaut badge, and the faith in the future of space exploration and continued desire to explore the universe that it stands for. The red, white and blue is for the national flags of the crew.

The five-pointed star on the mission patch represents the five space agencies involved with the ISS programme: NASA and the agencies of Russia, Europe, Japan and Canada. The triangular shape of the mission patch symbolizes the continued building of knowledge and experience from previous shuttle missions.

DID YOU KNOW?

During the STS-96 crew's time docked with the ISS, they spent more than 79 hours inside the space station and delivered over 3,500 pounds (1,600 kilograms) of supplies and logistics, including sleeping bags, clothing, medical equipment, spare parts, hardware and 84 US gallons (318 litres) of water.

Left to right: (back) Daniel Barry, Julie Payette, Valeri Tokarev, Tamara Jernigan; (front) Kent Rominger, Ellen Ochoa, Rick Husband

CREW

Eileen M. Collins – Commander
Jeffrey S. Ashby – Pilot
Michel Tognini – Mission Specialist (CNES)
Steven A. Hawley – Mission Specialist
Catherine G. 'Cady' Coleman – Mission Specialist

SPACECRAFT

Columbia, OV-102

LAUNCH DATE

23 July 1999

MISSION

• Deployment of Chandra X-Ray Observatory.

Left to right: Eileen Collins, Steven Hawley, Jeffrey Ashby, Michel Tognini, Cady Coleman

In this patch, designed by artist Mark Pestana, we see the Chandra X-Ray Observatory being deployed from Columbia, which leaves a green trajectory in its wake. The objectives of Chandra were to make astrophysical observations and study X-ray emissions from nebulae, stars and galaxies so scientists can learn more about the origins and evolution of the universe. A spiral galaxy can be seen in the background, which represents the types of celestial objects that Chandra would be investigating over the course of many years. The names of the five crew members are displayed around the patch, and the two national flags of the USA and France (for Michel Tognini) are featured above the orbiter. The final artwork for production was entrusted to NASA graphic designer Terry Johnson.

The crew conducted a series of experiments during the spaceflight using the Southwest Ultraviolet Imaging System (SWUIS), which took ultraviolet pictures of Earth, the Moon, Mercury, Venus and Jupiter. Other experiments included a biological cell culture experiment, plant growth and microgravity exercise observations using a treadmill.

DID YOU KNOW?

STS-93 was the first shuttle mission to have a female commander. Eileen Collins had previously been pilot on STS-63 and STS-84. She went on to be mission commander again on STS-114 in 2005.

CREW

Curtis L. Brown Jr – Commander
Scott J. Kelly – Pilot
John M. Grunsfeld – Mission Specialist
Jean-François Clervoy – Mission Specialist (ESA)
C. Michael Foale – Mission Specialist
Steven L. Smith – Mission Specialist
Claude Nicollier – Mission Specialist (ESA)

SPACECRAFT

Discovery, OV-103

LAUNCH DATE

19 December 1999

MISSION

• Third Hubble Space Telescope servicing mission.

STS-103 marked the third service-and-repair mission of the Hubble Space Telescope (HST). Designed by the crew of Discovery, the mission-patch artwork depicts the shuttle orbiting Earth and preparing to rendezvous with Hubble. Hubble is illustrated with its solar array panels fully extended and illuminated by the Sun, as seen on approach by the crews of previous servicing missions. During the spaceflight, three separate EVAs would be performed to replace some of Hubble's old systems with new, improved and more reliable ones. Repairs were also made to its exterior thermal insulation, which had suffered damage after nine years in space. The vertical and horizontal lines illustrated on HST represent its ability to reach and maintain a desired altitude in space, which is essential for the continued success of its mission. Once the crew had completed their tasks, Hubble was ready to get back to work exploring the far reaches of the solar system, distant galaxies and nebulae, and gaining insight into the origins of the universe.

The repair mission involved split EVAs, each of which lasted approximately eight hours. John Grunsfeld and Steven Smith conducted the first and third; Michael Foale and Claude Nicollier conducted EVA two. After all repairs had been completed, HST was redeployed from Discovery's payload bay on Christmas Day 1999.

Left to right: Michael Foale, Claude Nicollier, Scott Kelly, Curtis Brown, Jean-François Clervoy, John Grunsfeld, Steven Smith

STS-99

CREW

Kevin R. Kregel – Commander
Dominic L. Pudwill Gorie – Pilot
Gerhard P. J. Thiele – Mission Specialist (ESA)
Janet L. Kavandi – Mission Specialist
Janice E. Voss – Mission Specialist
Mamoru Mohri – Mission Specialist (NASDA)

SPACECRAFT

Endeavour, OV-105

LAUNCH DATE

11 February 2000

MISSION

• Shuttle Radar Topography Mission.

Left to right: (back) Janice Voss, Kevin Kregel,
Dominic Gorie, Janet Kavandi; (front) Mamoru Mohri,
Gerhard Thiele

This clean and stylish insignia – designed with creative input from all crew members – sees Endeavour carrying out Earth-mapping observations as part of the Shuttle Radar Topography Mission (SRTM) project, which is represented here by the grid over Earth. A 197-foot (60-metre) mast can be seen extending out from the shuttle's payload bay with a radar antenna at the tip; there is a second radar antenna located in the payload bay. The two yellow beams penetrate the atmosphere over Florida and the southeast coast of the USA to provide three-dimensional mapping data of Earth in a continued effort to understand our planet better. Earth's horizon is depicted as a rainbow, symbolizing a bright future for human space exploration.

Earth-mapping observations began just 12 hours into the flight, and the crew was split into two teams to allow continuous 24-hour working.

DID YOU KNOW?
After 11 days in space, the STS-99 crew had completed 222 hours and 23 minutes of mapping and filled 332 high-density tapes with radar imagery for detailed analysis back on Earth.

CREW

James D. Halsell Jr – Commander
Scott J. 'Doc' Horowitz – Pilot
Mary Ellen Weber – Mission Specialist
Jeffrey N. Williams – Mission Specialist
James S. Voss – Mission Specialist
Susan J. Helms – Mission Specialist
Yury V. Usachev – Mission Specialist (RKA)

SPACECRAFT

Atlantis, OV-104

LAUNCH DATE

19 May 2000

MISSION

• International Space Station Assembly Mission 2A.2a.

The STS-101 mission patch celebrates the collaborative nature of this third spaceflight to the International Space Station (ISS). Atlantis is featured on course to rendezvous and dock with the ISS in orbit. The ISS, which at this stage consisted of the American Unity module and Russian-built Zarya module, can be seen at the top of the insignia with Zarya's solar panels deployed. The two national flags of the USA and Russia feature in the border of the patch for this joint mission; the border itself is comprised of two trails, one from each craft. The American crew members, alongside Russia's Yury Usachev, are named in bold yellow text across the front. The three largest stars in the space scene tell us that this is the third mission to the International Space Station. Graphic artist David Russell worked with the crew to create the final artwork.

Atlantis delivered more than a ton of supplies to the ISS in preparation for the arrival of the ISS Expedition 1 crew later that year. James Voss and Jeffrey Williams conducted an EVA lasting almost seven hours to fit new hardware and external components in preparation for the docking of the Russian Zvezda Service Module, which arrived at the space station two months after the STS-101 mission.

Left to right: (back) Jeffrey Williams, James Voss; (middle) Mary Ellen Weber, Yuri Usachev, Susan J. Helms; (front) Doc Horowitz, James Halsell

CREW

Terrence W. Wilcutt – Commander
Scott D. Altman – Pilot
Edward T. Lu – Mission Specialist
Richard A. Mastracchio – Mission Specialist
Daniel C. Burbank – Mission Specialist
Yuri I. Malenchenko – Mission Specialist (RKA)
Boris V. Morukov – Mission Specialist (RKA)

SPACECRAFT

Atlantis, OV-104

LAUNCH DATE

September 2000

MISSION

International Space Station Assembly Mission 2A.2b.

Left to right: (back) Boris Morukov, Richard Mastracchio, Edward Lu, Daniel Burbank, Yuri Malenchenko; (front) Scott Altman, Terrence Wilcutt

On the STS-106 mission patch, Atlantis orbits Earth in preparation for docking with the International Space Station (ISS), with our planet shown as it would be seen from the crew's perspective. The ISS is at the bottom with the new Russian Zvezda Service Module connected at the back, as well as an automated Russian Progress cargo spacecraft (shown with the darker blue solar panels) beyond Zvezda. The gold astronaut emblem extends towards the shuttle as a symbol of the vital link between both spacecraft during the construction of the ISS and for future shuttle missions. The American and Russian flags are seen to join at the ISS in a statement of collaboration between the two nations in the construction of the ISS and to represent the bond between the Russian and American crews. The blue and gold of the border recall the colours of the US Marine Corps and US Navy, the services of mission commander Terrence Wilcutt and Scott Altman respectively.

The crew of STS-106 spent 11 days in space of which five were on the ISS, installing hardware and equipment inside the Zvezda Service Module and transferring supplies and logistics to the space station in preparation for the Expedition 1 crew. An EVA lasting more than six hours was conducted by Edward Lu and Yuri Malenchenko, installing power, data and communication cables between the new Zvezda module and Zarya module. A six-foot (1.8-metre) magnetometer was also fitted to the ISS to be used as a compass to show the station in relation to Earth.

CREW

Brian Duffy – Commander
Pamela A. Melroy – Pilot
Koichi Wakata – Mission Specialist (NASDA)
William S. McArthur – Mission Specialist
Peter J. K. 'Jeff' Wisoff – Mission Specialist
Michael E. López-Alegría – Mission Specialist
Leroy Chiao – Mission Specialist

SPACECRAFT

Discovery, OV-103

LAUNCH DATE

11 October 2000

MISSION

- International Space Station assembly mission 3A.
- 100th Space Shuttle mission.

The STS-92 patch is all about the International Space Station (ISS) assembly objectives of the mission. This was the second flight to deliver American-made components for installation onto the ISS. The dominant element of the patch is the silhouetted shuttle set against a dark-blue background. Central in the foreground, the ISS is depicted in its current configuration, which is, from bottom up: the US Unity module with its two Pressurized Mating Adapters (PAMs); the Russian Zarya functional cargo block; the Russian Zvezda Service Module; and the unpiloted Russian Progress cargo craft. The mission's main objective was to deliver and install the Zenith Z1 truss (in red to the right of the Unity module) and the third PAM (in red to the left of the Unity module). A large red Z behind the ISS symbolizes the Z1 truss; this then merges towards the top into a colourful version of the astronaut emblem.

After docking with the ISS on their second day in space, the crew began installation of the Z1 truss and PAM 3 to the Unity module. The five Discovery mission specialists conducted four separate EVAs to complete the assembly objectives in preparation for the arrival of the first ISS crew in November.

DID YOU KNOW?

STS-92 was the 100th launch of the Space Shuttle Program. By this time NASA shuttles, in five different incarnations, had been orbiting our planet for 19 years.

Left to right: (back) Leroy Chiao, Michael López-Alegría, William McArthur, Jeff Wisoff, Koichi Wakata; (front) Pamela Melroy, Brian Duffy

CREW

Brent W. Jett Jr – Commander
Michael J. Bloomfield – Pilot
Joseph R. Tanner – Mission Specialist
Marc Garneau – Mission Specialist (CSA)
Carlos I. Noriega – Mission Specialist

SPACECRAFT

Endeavour, OV-105

LAUNCH DATE

30 November 2000

MISSION

• International Space Station Assembly Mission 4A.
• Delivery and installation of P6 truss and solar arrays.

Here Endeavour is docked with the International Space Station (ISS) in low Earth orbit. The dominant features of the patch are the large gold solar arrays, which provide power to the station. They are part of the new P6 truss delivered and installed by the STS-97 crew. The P6 truss can be seen in silver (grey) attached to the Z1 truss that had been fitted during the STS-92 mission. The mission number is displayed against the blazing Sun, symbolizing the crew's pivotal role alongside our star in providing power to the ISS so a brand-new chapter can open in long-duration stays in space.

During the mission, Joseph Tanner and Carlos Noriega performed three separate EVAs, totalling over 19 hours, to add new components to the ISS. As well as the P6 truss and solar arrays, a docking port was prepared for the future arrival of the US Destiny laboratory module. A camera cable was fitted to the Unity module and floating potential probes were installed to measure electrical potential around the ISS. The crew also delivered fresh supplies and equipment to the station.

DID YOU KNOW?

The first ISS crew (Expedition 1) arrived on 2 November 2000 on a Russian Soyuz spacecraft, marking the beginning of a continuous human presence in space. ISS commander William M. Shepherd (NASA), Yuri P. Gidzenko and Sergei K. Krikalev (RKA) spent 136 days on board.

Left to right: (back) Carlos Noriega, Joseph Tanner;
(front) Michael Bloomfield, Marc Garneau, Brent Jett

STS-98

CREW

Kenneth D. Cockrell – Commander
Mark L. Polansky – Pilot
Robert L. Curbeam – Mission Specialist
Marsha S. Ivins – Mission Specialist
Thomas D. Jones – Mission Specialist

SPACECRAFT

Atlantis, OV-104

LAUNCH DATE

7 February 2001

MISSION

- International Space Station Assembly Mission 5A.
- Delivery and installation of the Destiny laboratory module.

STS-98's mission was to travel to the International Space Station (ISS) to deliver and install the American-built Destiny laboratory module, which was designed to provide future ISS crews with a revolutionary facility to conduct extensive and varied research. Atlantis is illustrated with its Remote Manipulator System robotic arm extended as it prepares to attach Destiny to the Unity module. Earth is reflected in Destiny's window. The constellation Hercules can be seen between the module and the orbiter; Hercules is a symbol of strength and a nod to the Herculean efforts of the shuttle and ISS crews. The patch is surrounded by the stars and stripes of the American flag, showing the country's continued commitment to the development of the ISS. This was the first shuttle insignia design to feature a gradient in the artwork since the STS-1 patch. Gradients were not part of the NASA art department guidelines due to production restrictions when manufacturing the embroidered versions. Artists Marc Jacobs and Terry Johnson worked on the final artwork for this insignia.

After Destiny had been secured in place, three EVAs were carried out to attach electrical, data and cooling cables to the laboratory, as well as other essentials such as handrails and sockets. Other assembly duties were conducted during the EVAs by Robert Curbeam and Thomas Jones, including the installation of a spare communications antenna to the exterior of the space station.

Left to right: (back) Robert Curbeam, Thomas Jones; (front) Mark Polansky, Marsha Ivins, Kenneth Cockrell

STS-102

CREW

James D. Wetherbee – Commander
James M. 'Vegas' Kelly – Pilot
Andrew S. W. Thomas – Mission Specialist
Paul W. Richards – Mission Specialist
Yury V. Usachev – ISS Expedition 2 'up' crew (RKA)
James S. Voss – ISS Expedition 2 'up' crew
Susan J. Helms – ISS Expedition 2 'up' crew
William M. Shepherd – ISS Expedition 1 'down' crew
Yuri P. Gidzenko – ISS Expedition 1 'down' crew (RKA)
Sergei K. Krikalev – ISS Expedition 1 'down' crew (RKA)

SPACECRAFT

Discovery, OV-103

LAUNCH DATE

8 March 2001

MISSION

- International Space Station Assembly Mission 5A.1.
- Rotation of ISS Expedition 1 and Expedition 2 crews.

Prime crew, left to right: Vegas Kelly, Andrew Thomas, James Wetherbee, Paul Richards

The STS-102 mission patch commemorates the first rotation of International Space Station (ISS) crews. On the first line of the bottom tab of the insignia are the names of the Expedition 2 crew who travelled on the shuttle to replace the Expedition 1 crew, named on line two, who had spent 136 days in space. The names of the four prime shuttle crew members can be seen running around the inside top of the patch. The rotation of ISS crews is symbolized by the looped red, white and blue ribbons encircling the station. The number 1 in the mission number is for the Expedition 1 crew, and the number 2 for Expedition 2. The 0 encircles the Destiny module in which the new crew will continue the work started by their predecessors.

The main focus of the patch is the view of the ISS as it would be seen by the shuttle crew on rendezvous and in preparation for docking, known as the 'V-bar approach'. During the mission, the Italian-built Leonardo Multi-Purpose Logistics Module was temporarily attached to the ISS to offload cargo, seen here at the bottom of the space station below the mission number. The national flags of Russia, the USA and Italy feature at the base of the patch, reminding us of the international nature of this flight and of the ISS. This assembly mission was designated 5A.1, which is represented by the star constellations to left and right of the ISS and the small letter A visible above the 0.

CREW

Kent V. Rominger – Commander
Jeffrey S. Ashby – Pilot
Chris A. Hadfield – Mission Specialist (CSA)
John L. Phillips – Mission Specialist
Scott E. Parazynski – Mission Specialist
Umberto Guidoni – Mission Specialist (ESA)
Yuri Lonchakov – Mission Specialist (RKA)

SPACECRAFT

Endeavour, OV-105

LAUNCH DATE

19 April 2001

MISSION

• International Space Station Assembly Mission 6A.

This International Space Station (ISS) assembly flight had the designation 6A as well as the shuttle designation STS-100, and both feature on the patch, which is shaped like an EVA space helmet. The primary objective of this mission was to deliver and install the Canadarm2 robotic arm to the ISS, seen at the bottom of the visor, connecting the two mission designations. Below Canadarm2 are the national flags of the crew members: the USA, Russia, Italy and Canada. Within the visor we see Endeavour with the ISS over Earth's horizon in the distance. As the Sun rises over Earth, Endeavour is illuminated and revealed to the station, emphasizing the unity of the two spacecraft and the central role the shuttle plays in making the ISS possible. Inside the shuttle's payload bay, towards the back, is the Italian-built Raffaello Multi-Purpose Logistics Module. In front of Raffaello is a Spacelab pallet containing the Canadarm2 and Space Station Ultra High Frequency Antenna that will be installed. The ten stars in the distance represent the children of the shuttle crew and symbolize the continued pursuit of exploring the universe long into the future.

STS-100 was the first spaceflight for the Raffaello Multi-Purpose Logistics Module. It was used to transfer 6,000 pounds (2,700 kilograms) of cargo to the ISS, including two new experiment racks for the Destiny laboratory and three US commercial payloads.

Left to right: (white suits) Scott Parazynski, Chris Hadfield; (orange suits) Yuri Lonchakov, Kent Rominger, Umberto Guidoni, Jeffrey Ashby, John Phillips

155

STS-104

CREW

Steven W. Lindsey – Commander
Charles O. Hobaugh – Pilot
Michael L. Gernhardt – Mission Specialist
Janet L. Kavandi – Mission Specialist
James F. Reilly II – Mission Specialist

SPACECRAFT

Atlantis, OV-104

LAUNCH DATE

12 July 2001

MISSION

• International Space Station Assembly Mission 7A.
• Installation of the Quest Joint Airlock.

Left to right: Michael Gernhardt, Charles Hobaugh,
Janet Kavandi, Steven Lindsey, James Reilly

Shuttle flight STS-104 was another assembly mission to the International Space Station (ISS), designated 7A, as shown on the insignia artwork. The primary objective was to deliver and install the Quest Joint Airlock, which can be seen at the back of the payload bay of Atlantis, where four high-pressure gas tanks containing nitrogen and oxygen have also been stowed. The Quest Joint Airlock is shown once more, this time attached to the ISS at the top right of the patch. The yellow astronaut emblem is featured behind and encircling the ISS and Atlantis, honouring the brave crews that have come before and the vital role of human spaceflight. The pentagon-shaped patch features the names of the five crew members in the blue border surrounding the stars and stripes of the US flag, showing America's commitment to the human space programme and the country's essential role in the future of space exploration. Graphic artist David Russell created the final artwork with creative direction from mission specialist Janet Kavandi.

The STS-100/7A mission marked the completion of the initial assembly phase of the ISS. James Reilly and Michael Gernhardt performed three EVAs to install the Quest Joint Airlock and other components. Supplies and equipment, including spacesuits, were transferred from the shuttle to the space station.

STS-105

CREW

Scott J. 'Doc' Horowitz – Commander
Frederick W. Sturckow – Pilot
Patrick G. Forrester – Mission Specialist
Daniel T. Barry – Mission Specialist
Frank L. Culbertson Jr – ISS Expedition 3 'up' crew
Vladimir N. Dezhurov – ISS Expedition 3 'up' crew (RKA)
Mikhail V. Tyurin – ISS Expedition 3 'up' crew (RKA)
Yury V. Usachev – ISS Expedition 2 'down' crew (RKA)
James S. Voss – ISS Expedition 2 'down' crew
Susan J. Helms – ISS Expedition 2 'down' crew

SPACECRAFT

Discovery, OV-103

LAUNCH DATE

10 August 2001

MISSION

• International Space Station Assembly Mission 7A.1.
• Rotation of ISS Expedition 2 and Expedition 3 crews.

The main objective of spaceflight STS-105 was the rotation of International Space Station (ISS) crews. In this patch – created by graphic artist David Russell and astronaut Pat Forrester – we see two shuttles in rotation to indicate the crew transfers and the continuous human presence in space. The ascending US-commanded Expedition 3 crew is represented by the shuttle trailing the US flag and the three stars beneath it; the Russian-commanded Expedition 2 crew returning to Earth are represented by the shuttle trailing the Russian flag and two stars above it. The two shuttles are linked by the astronaut emblem that marks the path between Earth and the ISS, the space station being shown as a star at the tip of the pin. The names of the four prime shuttle crew members encircle the patch, while the two ISS crews are displayed in the lower tab: line one 'up' and line two 'down'.

Discovery's payloads included the Early Ammonia Servicer (EAS), which was attached to the outside of the ISS, and the Leonardo Multi-Purpose Logistics Module, which was used to transfer 7,000 pounds (3,175 kilograms) of supplies, equipment and science racks to the ISS. Two EVAs were conducted, installing the EAS and fitting heater cables and handrails to the Destiny laboratory module.

Prime crew, left to right: Frederick Sturckow, Patrick Forrester, Daniel Barry, Doc Horowitz

STS-108

CREW

Dominic L. Pudwill Gorie – Commander
Mark E. Kelly – Pilot
Linda M. Godwin – Mission Specialist
Daniel M. Tani – Mission Specialist
Yuri I. Onufrienko – ISS Expedition 4 'up' crew (RKA)
Daniel W. Bursch – ISS Expedition 4 'up' crew
Carl E. Walz – ISS Expedition 4 'up' crew
Frank L. Culbertson Jr – ISS Expedition 3 'down' crew
Vladimir Dezhurov – ISS Expedition 3 'down' crew (RKA)
Mikhail V. Tyurin – ISS Expedition 3 'down' crew (RKA)

SPACECRAFT

Endeavour, OV-105

LAUNCH DATE

December 5, 2001

MISSION

• International Space Station Assembly Mission UF-1.
• Rotation of ISS Expedition 3 and Expedition 4 crews.

Prime crew, left to right: Mark Kelly, Linda Godwin,
Daniel Tani, Dominic Gorie

The STS-108 mission patch features the designation UF-1, marking this as the first Utilization Flight to the International Space Station (ISS). As Endeavour soars across the front of the insignia, the ISS is illustrated as it is seen by the shuttle crew during the final approach for docking. A primary mission objective was to deliver the Expedition 4 crew to the ISS and bring the Expedition 3 crew home. The Russian-commanded Expedition 4 crew is represented by the ascending trail (in the colour sequence of the Russian flag) from Earth to the ISS and three gold stars, one for each crew member; the US-commanded Expedition 3 crew is represented by the red, white and blue trail leaving the ISS and one gold star for each returning crew member. The four white stars are the four prime shuttle crew members who are responsible for the safe transfer of both crews, and their names are featured either side of the main design. In the tab at the bottom, the 'up' (line one) and 'down' (line two) ISS crews are named.

The shuttle carried the Raffaello Multi-Purpose Logistics Module inside its payload bay; this was temporarily attached to the station's Unity module to transfer new supplies and equipment over to the ISS. The Raffaello module was loaded with materials and returned to Endeavour's payload bay before the journey back to Earth.

CREW

Scott D. Altman – Commander
Duane G. Carey – Pilot
John M. Grunsfeld – Mission Specialist
Nancy J. Currie (née Sherlock) – Mission Specialist
Richard M. Linnehan – Mission Specialist
James H. Newman – Mission Specialist
Michael J. Massimino – Mission Specialist

SPACECRAFT

Columbia, OV-102

LAUNCH DATE

1 March 2002

MISSION

• Fourth Hubble Space Telescope servicing mission.

In the STS-109 design, we see Columbia rendezvousing with the Hubble Space Telescope high over the USA below. This was the fourth servicing mission undertaken to improve Hubble's performance and extend its lifespan. Here Hubble is pictured displaying the smaller, more efficient and more powerful solar array panels that were installed during this mission. The space scene in Hubble's aperture is known as the 'Hubble Deep Field', and it shows the spectacular celestial objects that Hubble is famous for photographing, such as distant galaxies and nebulae. After the crew had finished their service-and-upgrade mission objectives, Hubble could continue its investigations into the furthest reaches of the visible universe, relaying back to Earth the incredible and never-before-seen wonders of deep space. The design was conceived by the crew and graphic artist Sean Collins.

During a series of five EVAs conducted by astronauts Grunsfeld, Linnehan, Newman and Massimino, new equipment was installed in Hubble, including a new power control unit and an experimental cooling system.

DID YOU KNOW?
The Advanced Camera for Surveys, fitted by the STS-109 astronauts, would allow Hubble to capture twice the area with improved clarity and speed than it had previously.

Left to right: Michael Massimino, Richard Linnehan, Duane Carey, Scott Altman, Nancy Currie, John Grunsfeld, James Newman

CREW

Michael J. Bloomfield – Commander
Stephen N. Frick – Pilot
Rex J. Walheim – Mission Specialist
Ellen L. Ochoa – Mission Specialist
Lee M. E. Morin – Mission Specialist
Jerry L. Ross – Mission Specialist
Steven L. Smith – Mission Specialist

SPACECRAFT

Atlantis, OV-104

LAUNCH DATE

8 April 2002

MISSION

• International Space Station Assembly Mission 8A.
• Delivery and installation of the S0 truss segment.

Left to right: (back) Steven Smith, Rex Walheim,
Jerry Ross, Lee Morin; (front) Stephen Frick, Ellen Ochoa,
Michael Bloomfield

The STS-110 mission patch commemorates the start of the final phase of construction of the International Space Station (ISS). The crew of Atlantis delivered the S0 (Starboard 0) truss segment – the mission patch is actually shaped like the cross-section of the truss – to the ISS and installed it to the Destiny laboratory module. The S0 truss contains the navigational devices, computers, cooling and power systems needed to attach future modules to the space station and is used to send power to the ISS's pressurized modules and conduct heat away from them. The S0 truss is shown highlighted in yellow on the ISS at the top left of the design. Atlantis can be seen blasting upwards into orbit, leaving a trail of three fiery plumes behind it, marking the first shuttle flight to use three Block II Main Engines.

During the mission, four EVAs were performed to complete all assembly objectives, and the crew also transferred experiments and supplies between the shuttle and the station.

DID YOU KNOW?

During STS-110, Jerry Ross, on his final spaceflight, became the first person to venture into space seven times. Ross first flew on STS-61-B in 1985. He conducted nine spacewalks during his NASA career, totalling over 58 hours outside the spacecraft.

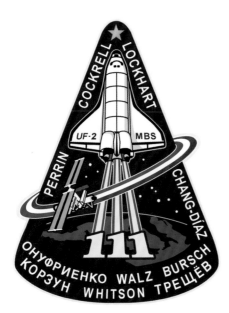

STS-111

CREW

Kenneth D. Cockrell – Commander
Paul S. Lockhart – Pilot
Philippe Perrin – Mission Specialist (CNES)
Franklin R. Chang-Díaz – Mission Specialist
Valery G. Korzun – ISS Expedition 5 'up' crew (RKA)
Peggy A. Whitson – ISS Expedition 5 'up' crew
Sergei Y. Treshchov – ISS Expedition 5 'up' crew (RKA)
Yuri I. Onufrienko – ISS Expedition 4 'down' crew (RKA)
Daniel W. Bursch – ISS Expedition 4 'down' crew
Carl E. Walz – ISS Expedition 4 'down' crew

SPACECRAFT

Endeavour, OV-105

LAUNCH DATE

5 June 2002

MISSION

• International Space Station Assembly Mission UF-2.
• Rotation of ISS Expedition 4 and Expedition 5 crews.

The inspiration for the layout and format of this mission-patch artwork is the astronaut badge. The design – created by artist Marc Jacobs and the crew – features Endeavour ascending towards space leaving a trail of three engine plumes that recall the badge, but also form the mission number 111. The International Space Station (ISS) is orbiting the shuttle, again recalling the badge design, leaving a trajectory in the shared colours of the national flags of each crew member: the USA, Russia, France and Costa Rica (the birth place of NASA astronaut Franklin Chang-Díaz). The gold star at the top of the patch is the final element that makes up the emblem, and it also represents the Johnson Space Center in Texas, the control centre for this mission. The shuttle carried supplies and equipment to the ISS via the Italian-built Leonardo Multi-Purpose Logistics Module, and Italy can be seen to the right of the plumes, so acknowledging this vital contribution to the flight. The letters MBS on the orbiter's right wing are for the Canadian Mobile Base System, which was delivered and installed onto the ISS; on the left wing we see the flight code UF-2: Utilization Flight-2. The ten stars are for the ten crew members who flew on Endeavour during this flight.

Endeavour delivered the Expedition 5 crew to the ISS and brought the Expedition 4 crew home. The two crews' names are at the bottom of the patch, while the prime crew are checked on the left and right borders of the upper section.

Prime crew, left to right: Philippe Perrin, Paul Lockhart, Kenneth Cockrell, Franklin Chang-Díaz

STS-112

STS-112

CREW

Jeffrey S. Ashby – Commander
Pamela A. Melroy – Pilot
Piers J. Sellers – Mission Specialist
Sandra H. Magnus – Mission Specialist
David A. Wolf – Mission Specialist
Fyodor N. Yurchikhin – Mission Specialist (RKA)

SPACECRAFT

Atlantis, OV-104

LAUNCH DATE

7 October 2002

MISSION

International Space Station Assembly Mission 9A.
Delivery and installation of the S1 truss segment.

Left to right: Sandra Magnus, David Wolf, Pamela Melroy,
Jeffrey Ashby, Piers Sellers, Fyodor Yurchikhin

STS-112 was the ninth assembly mission to the International Space Station (ISS). The designation 9A features in the centre of the patch along with the flight number 112 at the top. The primary mission objective was to deliver and install the S1 (Starboard 1) truss segment, and the patch design depicts the ISS as seen by the shuttle crew on departure, with the new S1 truss installed, shown in red. The shuttle's rendezvous trajectory is in yellow, and it meets the S1 truss with a large nine-pointed star to acknowledge the joint effort of the six shuttle and three ISS crew members in installing the truss. After completion, the trajectory continues around the ISS and ends at a six-pointed star for the six crew members of Atlantis. The octagonal patch is a reference to the shape of the cross-section of the Integrated Truss Structure, which forms the backbone of the ISS.

As well as the S1 truss, the shuttle also delivered Cart A of the Crew and Equipment Translation Aid (CETA), one of two powered carts that ride along the ISS to allow astronauts to carry out work on the station more efficiently. Three EVAs, totalling almost 20 hours, were conducted during the flight to complete all mission objectives.

CREW

James D. Wetherbee – Commander
Paul S. Lockhart – Pilot
Michael López-Alegría – Mission Specialist
John B. Herrington – Mission Specialist
Kenneth D. Bowersox – ISS Expedition 6 'up' crew
Nikolai M. Budarin – ISS Expedition 6 'up' crew (RKA)
Donald R. Pettit – ISS Expedition 6 'up' crew
Valery G. Korzun – ISS Expedition 5 'down' crew (RKA)
Peggy A. Whitson – ISS Expedition 5 'down' crew
Sergei Y. Treshchov – ISS Expedition 5 'down' crew (RKA)

SPACECRAFT

Endeavour, OV-105

LAUNCH DATE

23 November 2002

MISSION

• International Space Station Assembly Mission 11A.
• Rotation of ISS Expedition 5 and Expedition 6 crews.

A dominant feature in this design is the bold yellow depiction of the astronaut badge trailing through space, symbolizing the continued human presence in the stars and highlighting the achievements of space exploration. The insignia depicts Endeavour docked with the International Space Station (ISS), while the station's robotic arm transfers the P1 (Port 1) truss segment from the shuttle's payload bay ready for installation onto the ISS. The other primary objective was the transfer of the Expedition 6 crew to the ISS and the return of the Expedition 5 crew, whose names are featured in the bottom tab of the patch along with the US and Russian flags. The names of the four prime shuttle crew are displayed on the space station's large solar panels. The constellation Orion is visible at the top left of the artwork to represent the seven launching crew members of the spaceflight, while the three stars on the right are for the three ISS crew members who returned to Earth on the shuttle. The mission number 113 is featured in red Roman numerals below the ISS. David Russell – a graphic artist working for NASA – created the final artwork with creative direction from the crew.

The 14-day mission included three EVAs to install the new P1 truss to the ISS and conduct additional exterior duties. Endeavour transferred more than 2,500 pounds (1,100 kilograms) of supplies and equipment to the ISS.

Prime crew, left to right: Paul Lockhart, Michael López-Alegría, John Herrington, James Wetherbee

STS-107

CREW

Rick D. Husband – Commander
William C. McCool – Pilot
Michael P. Anderson – Payload Commander
David M. Brown – Mission Specialist
Kalpana Chawla – Mission Specialist
Laurel B. Clark – Mission Specialist
Ilan Ramon – Payload Specialist (ISA)

SPACECRAFT

Columbia, OV-102

LAUNCH DATE

16 January 2003

MISSION

- Microgravity science research with SPACEHAB module.
- Columbia broke apart during re-entry, resulting in the loss of the shuttle and claiming the lives of all seven crew members.

Left to right: David Brown, Rick Husband, Laurel Clark, Kalpana Chawla, Michael Anderson, William McCool, Ilan Ramon

The STS-107 mission patch is in the iconic shape of the Space Shuttle itself, the only patch ever to be designed in that format. The dominant feature here is the microgravity symbol, µg, which merges into the iconic gold astronaut emblem, and this is a nod to the microgravity-research objectives of this 16-day flight. The sunrise also heralds the new era in microgravity research in space. Columbia was launched on a 39-degree inclination orbit, referenced by the angle of the astronaut emblem to Earth's horizon. The stars and Earth remind us of the vital role human space exploration has in pushing the boundaries of science, which will benefit all the world's people. Artist Richard Dann sketched the design for the insignia at the request of Kalpana Chawla. The final version was created by NASA artist Terry Johnson with creative guidance from Laurel Clark. The seven crew members are represented by the seven stars of the constellation Columba (the Dove), as a symbol of peace on Earth and a reference to the name Columbia; they are also a tribute to the original pioneering Mercury 7 astronauts. Payload specialist Ilan Ramon was the first Israeli astronaut, a fact acknowledged by the inclusion of the Israeli flag and a subtly placed Star of David within the constellation Columba.

DID YOU KNOW?

On 1 February 2003, Columbia broke apart while re-entering Earth's atmosphere, and all seven crew members lost their lives. The disaster was caused by a piece of foam that broke off the external fuel tank during launch, damaging the shuttle's heat shield on its left wing.

STS-114

CREW

Eileen M. Collins – Commander
James M. 'Vegas' Kelly – Pilot
Soichi Noguchi – Mission Specialist (JAXA)
Stephen K. Robinson – Mission Specialist
Andrew S. W. Thomas – Mission Specialist
Wendy B. Lawrence – Mission Specialist
Charles J. Camarda – Mission Specialist

SPACECRAFT

Discovery, OV-103

LAUNCH DATE

26 July 2005

MISSION

• 'Return-to-flight' mission.
• International Space Station Assembly Mission LF1.

After the loss of STS-107, the Space Shuttle Program was grounded for two and a half years. For this 'return-to-flight' mission, also known as Logistics Flight 1 (LF1), the insignia honours the fallen crew of Columbia with the seven stars of the constellation Columba that featured on the STS-107 patch. The main element in this design is a stylized planet Earth, symbolizing the contributions to the International Space Station (ISS) from space agencies around the world, including their support in improving the safety of spaceflight to make human space exploration possible. The blue ring represents the orbital trajectory of the ISS; the names of the three astronauts who would conduct EVAs while docked with the ISS are displayed here, with a red dot referencing the Japanese flag for Soichi Noguchi. Graphic artist Sean Collins worked closely with the crew to create the final artwork.

STS-107 delivered supplies to the ISS using the Raffaello Multi-Purpose Logistics Module and conducted shuttle-repair investigations. The shuttle's colourful trail recognizes the broad spectrum of mission objectives.

DID YOU KNOW?

After the tragic loss of the Columbia crew on STS-107, new procedures were put in place to examine the orbiters while in space. Eileen Collins was the first astronaut to fly the shuttle in a 360-degree pitch manoeuvre so the ISS crew could photograph the shuttle's heat shield and any damages could be assessed by mission control before re-entry was deemed safe.

Left to right: Stephen Robinson, Vegas Kelly, Andrew Thomas, Wendy Lawrence, Charles Camarda, Eileen Collins, Soichi Noguchi

STS-121

CREW

Steven W. Lindsey – Commander
Mark E. Kelly – Pilot
Michael E. Fossum – Mission Specialist
Lisa M. Nowak – Mission Specialist
Stephanie D. Wilson – Mission Specialist
Piers J. Sellers – Mission Specialist
Thomas A. Reiter – ISS Expedition 13 'up' crew (ESA)

SPACECRAFT

Discovery, OV-103

LAUNCH DATE

4 July 2006

MISSION

- International Space Station Assembly Mission ULF 1.1.
- Astronaut Thomas Reiter joins the ISS crew.

Left to right: Thomas Reiter, Michael Fossum, Piers Sellers,
Steven Lindsey, Mark Kelly, Stephanie Wilson, Lisa Nowak

STS-121, also known as Utilization and Logistics Flight 1.1, was the final
'return-to-flight' mission after the STS-107 disaster, and the sunrise that can
be seen breaking over Earth's horizon celebrates the start of this new era in
ISS–shuttle operations. The mission-patch design features Discovery docked
with the International Space Station (ISS) during this resupply mission,
while the gold astronaut emblem backdrops the two craft, reiterating the
importance and significance of a continued human presence in space.

The shuttle delivered 7,400 pounds (3,350 kilograms) of supplies, equipment
and experiments to the ISS via the Leonardo Multi-Purpose Logistics
Module, which was attached to the station's Unity module. New orbital
replacement units (ORUs) were delivered and stored on the station's exterior.
These ORUs consisted of backup pumps, storage tanks, controller boxes,
antennae and battery units for the ISS. Extensive photography of the orbiter
was conducted throughout the mission, and new techniques were also
tested for shuttle damage inspection and repair duties while in orbit.

DID YOU KNOW?
*STS-121 delivered German astronaut Thomas Reiter to begin his stay on
board the ISS as part of the Expedition 13/14 crew, the first three-person
crew on the space station since 2003.*

STS-115 marked the resumption of assembly missions to the International Space Station (ISS) after a four-year hiatus. The primary objective was to deliver and install the P3/P4 (Port 3 and Port 4) truss segment, which housed the station's two new solar array panels. The mission-patch artwork depicts Atlantis launching over a large solar panel. As the shuttle lifts off it leaves a trail reminiscent of an astronaut badge. A blazing, six-pointed sunrise breaks over the bright-blue Earth, symbolizing the six crew members of Atlantis and the source of energy that the ISS harnesses to allow continuous scientific research in microgravity. The 12 smaller rays mark the 12th American assembly mission to the ISS, also referenced at the bottom of the patch. The shuttle's destination, the ISS, can be seen in the distance along with six prominent stars, one for each member of the crew of Atlantis. The mission patch – created by Graham Huber, Gigi Lui and Peter Hui – was chosen from a selection of designs submitted by students of York University in Toronto, Canada. Terry Johnson, a graphic artist working for NASA, created the final artwork for production from the original coloured pencil drawing.

The P3/P4 truss segment was deployed from the payload bay using the shuttle's robotic arm and transferred to the ISS's own robotic arm. Three EVAs were conducted to install the truss segment and deploy the new solar panels, which have a wingspan of 240 feet (73 metres).

STS-115

CREW

Brent W. Jett Jr – Commander
Christopher J. Ferguson – Pilot
Steven G. MacLean – Mission Specialist (CSA)
Daniel C. Burbank – Mission Specialist
Joseph R. Tanner – Mission Specialist
Heidemarie M. Stefanyshyn-Piper – Mission Specialist

SPACECRAFT

Atlantis, OV-104

LAUNCH DATE

9 September 2006

MISSION

- International Space Station Assembly Mission 12A.
- Delivery and installation of the P3/P4 truss and solar arrays.

Left to right: Heidemarie Stefanyshyn-Piper, Christopher Ferguson, Joseph Tanner, Daniel Burbank, Brent Jett, Steven MacLean

STS-116

CREW

Mark L. Polansky – Commander
William A. Oefelein – Pilot
Nicholas J. M. Patrick – Mission Specialist
Robert L. Curbeam Jr – Mission Specialist
A. Christer Fuglesang – Mission Specialist (ESA)
Joan E. Higginbotham – Mission Specialist
Sunita Williams – ISS Expedition 14 'up' crew
Thomas A. Reiter – ISS Expedition 14 'down' crew (ESA)

SPACECRAFT

Discovery, OV-103

LAUNCH DATE

9 December 2006

MISSION

- International Space Station Assembly Mission 12A.1.
- Delivery and installation of the P5 truss segment.
- Rotation of ISS crew members Williams and Reiter.

Left to right: Robert Curbeam, William Oefelein,
Nicholas Patrick, Joan Higginbotham, Suni Williams,
Mark Polansky, Christer Fuglesang

Here we see Discovery orbiting high above Earth and the International Space Station (ISS). The national flags of the USA and Sweden form the shuttle's trail for the six Americans and one Swede in the launching crew. The primary objective of this assembly mission to the ISS was the delivery of the P5 (Port 5) truss segment, which was installed during the first of four EVAs that were undertaken. The seven stars of the constellation Ursa Major, otherwise known as the Big Dipper or the Plough, appear on the left-hand side of the patch and represent the seven launching crew members. The constellation has long been used to help locate the brightest star in the sky, the North Star, referenced here by the glowing star on the ISS, which is positioned where the P5 truss would be fitted, thus acknowledging the primary mission objective. The North Star has eight points, which stand for the eight crew members in total to fly on the shuttle during STS-116. Suni Williams, whose name appears in the tab at the bottom, replaced Thomas Reiter as part of the ISS crew.

EVAs were conducted to install components to the ISS and rewire the station's electrical power system. The crew of Discovery also transferred more than two tons of food, water and equipment for the ISS crew as well as transferring waste, used equipment and experiments back into the shuttle's cargo module for return to Earth.

STS-117

CREW

Frederick W. Sturckow – Commander
Lee J. Archambault – Pilot
Patrick G. Forrester – Mission Specialist
Steven R. Swanson – Mission Specialist
John D. 'Danny' Olivas – Mission Specialist
James F. Reilly II – Mission Specialist
Clayton C. Anderson – ISS Expedition 15 'up' crew
Sunita Williams – ISS Expedition 15 'down' crew

SPACECRAFT

Atlantis, OV-104

LAUNCH DATE

8 June 2007

MISSION

- International Space Station Assembly Mission 13A.
- Delivery of the S3/S4 truss and solar arrays.
- Rotation of ISS crew members Anderson and Williams.

The STS-117 artwork – created by artist David Russell with astronaut Pat Forrester – features the International Space Station (ISS) in orbit over Earth. This was another assembly flight to the ISS, to deliver and install the S3/S4 (Starboard 3/4) truss segment, which included a new set of solar array panels, seen highlighted in gold in the patch design. Atlantis bursts through the top of the mission patch, flanked by the stars and stripes of the US flag, symbolizing America's ongoing commitment to the ISS project and human space exploration. The mission number, 117, at the base of the patch has a stylized gold astronaut emblem either side, representing the efforts of all crew members, past and present, in the construction of the ISS.

The names of the commander and pilot of STS-117 are featured above the ISS, and the mission specialists are listed below. During the mission, Clayton Anderson was transferred to the space station, replacing Suni Williams as part of the ISS Expedition 15 crew.

DID YOU KNOW?

The launch of STS-117 was held back following a severe thunderstorm over Kennedy Space Center in February 2007 while the shuttle was on the launch pad. Large hailstones caused damage to the external tank's foam insulation as well as some of the shuttle's protective heat-shield tiles. Atlantis had to be rolled back to the Vehicle Assembly Building to allow repairs to be carried out.

Left to right: Clayton Anderson, James Reilly, Steven Swanson, Frederick Sturckow, Lee Archambault, Patrick Forrester, Danny Olivas

STS-118

CREW

Scott J. Kelly – Commander
Charles O. Hobaugh – Pilot
Tracy E. Caldwell Dyson – Mission Specialist
Richard A. Mastracchio – Mission Specialist
Dafydd R. 'Dave' Williams – Mission Specialist (CSA)
Barbara R. Morgan – Mission Specialist
B. Alvin Drew – Mission Specialist

SPACECRAFT

Endeavour, OV-105

LAUNCH DATE

8 August 2007

MISSION

• International Space Station Assembly Mission 13A.1.
• Delivery and installation of the S5 truss segment.

Left to right: Richard Mastracchio, Barbara Morgan,
Charles Hobaugh, Scott Kelly, Tracy Caldwell Dyson,
Dave Williams, Alvin Drew

The delivery and installation of the S5 (Starboard 5) truss segment to the International Space Station (ISS) was the primary objective of STS-118. Endeavour is seen orbiting Earth, leaving a trail composed of the US flag, and the seven stars in the trail are for the crew members of the shuttle. The gold astronaut emblem is seen reaching towards the ISS having been circled by the shuttle, and the star at the tip pinpoints the location of the S5 truss segment once installed. The left-hand section of the patch features a flame of knowledge to honour teachers, students and the power of education. The crew's names are displayed around the border, and a red maple leaf accompanies that of Canadian mission specialist Dave Williams.

Through a series of four spacewalks, crew members installed many other additional components to the ISS, including a gyroscope onto the Z1 segment of the station's truss, the external stowage platform 3 and the External Wireless Instrumentation System antenna. STS-118 was the final flight to carry the SPACEHAB module inside the shuttle's payload bay.

STS-120

CREW

Pamela A. Melroy – Commander
George D. Zamka – Pilot
Douglas H. Wheelock – Mission Specialist
Stephanie D. Wilson – Mission Specialist
Scott E. Parazynski – Mission Specialist
Paolo A. Nespoli – Mission Specialist (ESA)
Daniel M. Tani – ISS Expedition 16 'up' crew
Clayton C. Anderson – ISS Expedition 16 'down' crew

SPACECRAFT

Discovery, OV-103

LAUNCH DATE

23 October 2007

MISSION

- International Space Station Assembly Mission 10A.
- Delivery of the Harmony Node 2 module.
- Repositioning of the P6 truss and solar arrays.
- Rotation of ISS crew members Tani and Anderson.

The STS-120 mission patch – designed by graphic artist Marc Jacobs and the crew – features a golden Discovery high above Earth, with its trail forming the plumes of the astronaut emblem. The gold swirl maps the trajectory of the flight from launch to docking with the International Space Station (ISS) and is also a number 6 in honour of the six prime crew members on the shuttle. The crew's main objective was to deliver and install the Harmony Node 2 module, illustrated here inside the shuttle. Another task was to reposition the solar arrays of the P6 truss. The bright star on the left is the ISS, with the two red points representing the position of the solar array before being moved. Once repositioned to the port end (P5 truss) of the Integrated Truss Structure, the new position is marked by the two gold points.

The Moon, Mars and the constellation Orion (beneath the shuttle) were placed in the design to celebrate NASA's Constellation programme, which planned to send human crews back to the moon by 2020 and eventually onto Mars using an Orion spacecraft. The programme was cancelled in 2009 following budget cuts.

DID YOU KNOW?

Pamela Melroy was the second woman to command a shuttle mission. On arrival at the ISS, STS-120 was greeted by a crew headed by Peggy Whitson, the first female commander of the space station.

Left to right: Scott Parazynski, Douglas Wheelock, Stephanie Wilson, George Zamka, Pamela Melroy, Daniel Tani, Paolo Nespoli

STS-122

CREW

Stephen N. Frick – Commander
Alan G. Poindexter – Pilot
Leland D. Melvin – Mission Specialist
Rex J. Walheim – Mission Specialist
Hans W. Schlegel – Mission Specialist (ESA)
Stanley G. Love – Mission Specialist
Léopold Eyharts – ISS Expedition 16 'up' crew (ESA)
Daniel M. Tani – ISS Expedition 16 'down' crew

SPACECRAFT

Atlantis, OV-104

LAUNCH DATE

7 February 2008

MISSION

- International Space Station Assembly Mission 1E.
- Delivery of the European science laboratory, Columbus.
- Rotation of ISS crew members Eyharts and Tani.

Left to right: Leland Melvin, Stephen Frick, Rex Walheim,
Léopold Eyharts, Stanley Love, Alan Poindexter,
Hans Schlegel

The insignia for the STS-122 mission – also known as ISS-1E by the International Space Station (ISS) crew – makes a connection between the great sea voyages of the past and contemporary exploration of the universe. At the bottom right we see a 15th-century sailing vessel, of the kind that first crossed the Atlantic from Europe to the New World, notably that of Christopher Columbus; Atlantis is illustrated continuing that journey connected to the ship by a trail that recalls the astronaut badge. The primary objective of this mission was to deliver the European Space Agency's Columbus science laboratory to the ISS. The six stars shown in the main section of the mission patch represent the six prime crew members of Atlantis. The two stars that accompany the ISS designation 1E suggest a reference to the two crew members who were to remain on board the space station during crew transfer. The star underneath the mission number 122 is for the 'up' crew member staying in space, and the star pictured bottom left is for the 'down' crew member going home.

Other payloads delivered to the ISS included the BioLab Biological Experiment Laboratory, the Fluid Science Laboratory, the European Drawer Rack, the European Physiology Modules, the Solar Monitoring Observatory (SOLAR) and the European Technology Exposure Facility (EuTEF).

CREW

Dominic L. Pudwill Gorie – Commander
Gregory H. Johnson – Pilot
Robert L. Behnken – Mission Specialist
Michael J. Foreman – Mission Specialist
Richard M. Linnehan – Mission Specialist
Takao Doi – Mission Specialist (JAXA)
Garrett E. Reisman – ISS Expedition 16 'up' crew
Léopold Eyharts – ISS Expedition 16 'down' crew (ESA)

SPACECRAFT

Endeavour, OV-105

LAUNCH DATE

11 March 2008

MISSION

- International Space Station Assembly Mission 1J/A.
- Delivery of the first module for the Japanese Experiment Module, Kibo.
- Rotation of ISS crew members Reisman and Eyharts.

The STS-123 patch design focuses on the primary payloads delivered to the International Space Station (ISS) on this 15-day assembly mission. Endeavour is illustrated lifting the Japanese Experiment Logistics Module-Pressurized Section (ELM-PS) – the first module of the Japanese Experiment Module (JEM), also known as Kibo – with its robotic arm. The shuttle also delivered the Canadian-built Dextre robotics system (Special Purpose Dexterous Manipulator), seen fully assembled on the left with its maple-leaf badge. The ISS is shown in the distance. Like so many mission patches before it, this one makes use of the astronaut emblem as a core element. The three gold rocket plumes and star intersect the scene, while the shuttle's trajectory draws the orbital ring that encircles the design. The mission commander and pilot are named in the gold section of the flight path, while the names of the other five astronauts who launched on STS-123 are shown in the red section. Artist Mark Pestana designed the patch, with revisions and final production artwork by Sean Collins.

The stars in the design represent all crew members who flew on this mission. The two closest to the shuttle's flight deck stand for the commander and pilot. The three scattered around Dextre are the three mission specialists – Linnehan, Foreman and Behnken – who conducted EVAs to assemble the unit. The star to the left of Kibo is Takao Doi, the Japanese astronaut on the flight. The star beside the ISS is Garrett Reisman, who joined the ISS crew, and the yellow star is Léopold Eyharts, who returned to Earth on the shuttle after more than six weeks on the ISS.

Left to right: (back) Richard Linnehan, Robert Behnken, Garrett Reisman, Michael Foreman, Takao Doi; (front) Gregory Johnson, Dominic Gorie

STS-124

CREW

Mark E. Kelly – Commander
Kenneth T. Ham – Pilot
Karen L. Nyberg – Mission Specialist
Ronald J. Garan Jr – Mission Specialist
Michael E. Fossum – Mission Specialist
Akihiko Hoshide – Mission Specialist (JAXA)
Gregory E. Chamitoff – ISS Expedition 17 'up' crew
Garrett E. Reisman – ISS Expedition 17 'down' crew

SPACECRAFT

Discovery, OV-103

LAUNCH DATE

31 May 2008

MISSION

- International Space Station Assembly Mission 1J.
- Delivery of the Pressurized Module and Japanese Remote Manipulator System for Kibo.
- Rotation of ISS crew members Chamitoff and Reisman.

Left to right: Gregory Chamitoff, Michael Fossum,
Kenneth Ham, Mark Kelly, Karen Nyberg, Ronald Garan,
Akihiko Hoshide

The STS-124 mission patch celebrates the continued assembly of the Japanese Experiment Module, known as Kibo ('hope' in English), on the International Space Station (ISS). The artwork features Discovery docked with the Harmony module, exposing its black heat shield. The Columbus module is visible to the left of Harmony, and Kibo's Experiment Logistics Module-Pressurized Section (ELM-PS), which was delivered during STS-123, is shown attached to the top of Harmony. The primary mission objective was to deliver the core section of Kibo, the Japanese Experiment Module-Pressurized Module (JEM-PM). The mission patch sees the JEM-PM being lifted from Discovery's payload bay by the ISS's robotic arm prior to being attached to the right-hand side of Harmony. Once connected, the ELM-PS would be placed in its permanent position on top of the JEM-PM. The US flag adorns the top of the patch, and Japan's vital contribution to the mission is represented by the Japanese flag on the JEM-PM and the name Kibo written in Japanese characters at the bottom of the patch. The sun beating down on Earth is designed to resemble the traditional Rising Sun flag of Japan, symbolizing hope for the future of humankind and the benefits that will result from research from Kibo. The artwork was created by Perry Jackson with guidance from astronaut Ron Garan and the crew.

During the 14-day mission, nine of which were spent docked with the ISS, the crew performed external maintenance operations of the station and outfitted Kibo with supplies and equipment. The crew also delivered and installed the Japanese Remote Manipulator System robotic arm onto Kibo.

CREW

Christopher J. Ferguson – Commander
Eric A. Boe – Pilot
Donald R. Pettit – Mission Specialist
Stephen G. Bowen – Mission Specialist
Heidemarie M. Stefanyshyn-Piper – Mission Specialist
Robert S. Kimbrough – Mission Specialist
Sandra H. Magnus – ISS Expedition 18 'up' crew
Gregory E. Chamitoff – ISS Expedition 18 'down' crew

SPACECRAFT

Endeavour, OV-105

LAUNCH DATE

14 November 2008

MISSION

• International Space Station Assembly mission ULF2.
• Rotation of ISS crew members Magnus and Chamitoff.

This STS-126 patch was designed by artists Tim Gagnon and Jorge Cartes with creative direction from pilot Eric Boe and the crew of STS-126. It was designed in the shape of the Leonardo Multi-Purpose Logistics Module transported inside Endeavour's payload bay. The module, which on this flight carried new experiments, life-support racks and additional crew quarters, was used to transfer supplies and equipment to the International Space Station (ISS), allowing larger crews to complete longer-duration stays. The insignia's blue and gold colour scheme symbolizes the US Navy background of mission commander Christopher Ferguson and the gold astronaut emblem sits at the top of the design in celebration of human space exploration. The artwork illustrates Endeavour's flight path to the ISS and its triumphant return to Earth with a yellow trail, which also contains the mission designation. While docked with the ISS, the crew conducted EVAs to service and repair the Solar Alpha Rotary Joints of the solar arrays, the large panels that provide power to the ISS. This is referenced with a blazing sunrise peering over Earth's horizon, providing the essential power to the newly serviced solar panels.

The constellation Orion to the right of the shuttle represents NASA's intention to return humans to the Moon and eventually Mars using the newly developed Orion spacecraft. The Moon (left of Endeavour) and Mars (top right) are included to herald America's future space voyages.

Left to right: Heidemarie Stefanyshyn-Piper, Robert Kimbrough, Eric Boe, Christopher Ferguson, Stephen Bowen, Sandra Magnus, Donald Pettit

STS-119

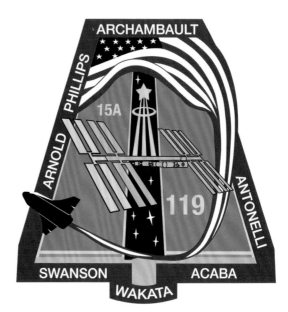

CREW

Lee J. Archambault – Commander
Dominic A. 'Tony' Antonelli – Pilot
Joseph M. Acaba – Mission Specialist
Steven R. Swanson – Mission Specialist
Richard R. Arnold II – Mission Specialist
John L. Phillips – Mission Specialist
Koichi Wakata – ISS Expedition 18 'up' crew (JAXA)
Sandra H. Magnus – ISS Expedition 18 'down' crew

SPACECRAFT

Discovery, OV-103

LAUNCH DATE

15 March 2009

MISSION

- International Space Station Assembly Mission 15A.
- Delivery and installation of S6 truss and solar arrays.
- Rotation of ISS crew members Wakata and Magnus.

Left to right: (back) Joseph Acaba, John Phillips,
Steven Swanson, Richard Arnold, Koichi Wakata;
(front) Tony Antonelli, Lee Archambault

STS-119 ferried the final set of solar array panels to the International Space Station (ISS), and to commemorate this event the mission patch was designed to resemble a solar array consisting of two blue panels. The ISS is featured across the middle of the patch with the new S6 (Starboard 6) truss segment and solar panels highlighted in yellow. The astronaut emblem rises up above the ISS, representing the dedication of the crews to a continued presence in space. The two mission designations – ISS and shuttle – are displayed one on each panel. The mission also delivered Japanese astronaut Koichi Wakata to the ISS as part of the Expedition 18 crew. The stars down the middle of the patch are the crew, and Wakata is also acknowledged individually by the red Sun of the Japanese flag displayed on the Kibo module on the ISS. The 17 white stars in the insignia remember the crews of Apollo 1, STS-51L and STS-107, all of whom lost their lives in the pursuit of space exploration. Discovery soars around the mission patch leaving a trail of stars and stripes in recognition of the support the American people have given to NASA's Space Shuttle Program.

Three separate EVAs were conducted, during which the new solar arrays were installed, some station maintenance was undertaken (including fitting additional foot grips to benefit future EVAs) and a new Global Positioning Satellite antenna was attached to the Kibo module.

CREW

Scott D. Altman – Commander
Gregory C. Johnson – Pilot
Michael T. Good – Mission Specialist
K. Megan McArthur – Mission Specialist
John M. Grunsfeld – Mission Specialist
Michael J. Massimino – Mission Specialist
Andrew J. Feustel – Mission Specialist

SPACECRAFT

Atlantis, OV-104

LAUNCH DATE

11 May 2009

MISSION

• Fifth and final shuttle flight to service the Hubble
Space Telescope.

The STS-125 mission-patch design – by renowned *Star Trek* graphic artist Michael Okuda – illustrates Atlantis rocketing through space during the fifth and final mission to service the Hubble Space Telescope. The crew conducted five EVAs to make repairs and install two new instruments, the Cosmic Origins Spectrograph and the Wide Field Camera 3. These upgrades allowed Hubble to provide a more detailed and wider view of the universe and the phenomenon known as dark matter or dark energy, represented here by the dominant black background. Hubble is at the bottom of the design, projecting stars and galaxies in its widened field of vision. The crew of Atlantis are named around the patch, which is outlined by a red border to suggest the redshift present in the light of very distant celestial objects as they move further away. Graphic artist Terry Johnson produced the final artwork with John Grunsfeld.

The maintenance work and addition of new hardware during the mission extended Hubble's lifespan and allowed the telescope to continue to provide awe-inspiring images of the universe for years to come.

DID YOU KNOW?

The Hubble Space Telescope is 43½ feet (13.3 metres) in length. It takes approximately 95 minutes to complete one orbit of Earth travelling at a speed of 17,000 mph (27,300 kph). From a low-Earth orbit altitude of approximately 350 miles (565 kilometres), Hubble can observe astronomical objects more than 13 billion light years away from Earth.

Left to right: Michael Massimino, Michael Good, Gregory Johnson, Scott Altman, Megan McArthur, John Grunsfeld, Andrew Feustel

STS-127

CREW

Mark L. Polansky – Commander
Douglas G. Hurley – Pilot
Christopher J. Cassidy – Mission Specialist
Julie Payette – Mission Specialist (CSA)
Thomas H. Marshburn – Mission Specialist
David A. Wolf – Mission Specialist
Timothy L. Kopra – ISS Expedition 20 'up' crew
Koichi Wakata – ISS Expedition 20 'down' crew (JAXA)

SPACECRAFT

Endeavour, OV-105

LAUNCH DATE

15 July 2009

MISSION

- International Space Station Assembly Mission 2J/A.
- Delivery of the final two components for Kibo.
- Rotation of ISS crew members Kopra and Wakata.

Left to right: David Wolf, Christopher Cassidy,
Douglas Hurley, Julie Payette, Mark Polansky,
Thomas Marshburn, Timothy Kopra

This simple yet elegant design – created by artists Tim Gagnon and Jorge Cartes with guidance from astronaut Tom Marshburn – commemorates the final mission to complete the assembly of the Japanese Experiment Module, Kibo. The shuttle crew delivered and installed the Japanese Experiment Module-Exposed Facility (JEM-EF) and Experiment Logistics Module-Exposed Section (ELM-ES) to the International Space Station (ISS). The patch illustrates the trajectory of Endeavour, which begins to form the iconic astronaut emblem in front of the orbiting shuttle. The gold star at the tip of the emblem references the same design used on the Japanese Space Agency logo. The crescent Earth is illuminated on one side and without a boundary line to symbolize that our planet is shared by all humankind. The ten stars against the blackness of space represent the ten astronauts in orbit at the time of the mission: the seven launching crew members of STS-127, the two crew members of the ISS and the third ISS crew member who returned to Earth on the shuttle. The crew members' names encircle the patch, with Canadian astronaut Julie Payette distinguished by the red maple leaf of the Canadian flag.

Endeavour was docked with the ISS for 11 days during the 16-day spaceflight. Five separate EVAs were performed during the mission by Kopra, Wolf, Marshburn and Cassidy to complete the installation of Kibo as well as many other tasks, including battery replacement on the P6 truss solar array section of the ISS.

CREW

Frederick W. Sturckow – Commander
Kevin A. Ford – Pilot
Patrick G. Forrester – Mission Specialist
José M. Hernández – Mission Specialist
John D. Olivas – Mission Specialist
A. Christer Fuglesang – Mission Specialist (ESA)
Nicole M. P. Stott – ISS Expedition 20 'up' crew
Timothy L. Kopra – ISS Expedition 20 'down' crew

SPACECRAFT

Discovery, OV-103

LAUNCH DATE

28 August 2009

MISSION

• International Space Station Assembly Mission 17A.
• Rotation of ISS crew members Stott and Kopra.

STS-128 was a mission to deliver fresh supplies and new equipment to the International Space Station (ISS), and the Leonardo Multi-Purpose Logistics Module, which carried life-support racks, new experiments and science equipment to the ISS, can be seen secured in Discovery's payload bay. The central element of the design is the gold astronaut emblem that forms the backdrop for the patch and serves as a tribute to the continued human presence in space and the courageous men and women who embark upon these voyages. The Florida launch site is visible on the globe, and the shuttle's trajectory can be seen lifting off from there and arriving at the ISS. The names of the mission commander and pilot are displayed at the top, followed by the mission specialists' names within the banner surrounding the patch. Nicole Stott travelled to the ISS to become part of the Expedition 20/21 crew, and she is named at the bottom of the artwork. The mission number is displayed in the gold section of the banner, which also forms the orbital ring that completes the astronaut emblem. The national flags of Sweden (Fuglesang) and the USA (all the other crew members) feature on either side of the insignia. Graphic designer David Russell created the artwork for the patch alongside mission specialist Pat Forrester.

The mission lasted 14 days with nine of those docked with the ISS. Three separate ISS assembly and maintenance EVAs were conducted during that time by Stott, Olivas and Fuglesang.

Left to right: José Hernández, Kevin Ford, John Olivas, Nicole Stott, Christer Fuglesang, Frederick Sturckow, Patrick Forrester

STS-129

CREW

Charles O. Hobaugh – Commander
Barry E. 'Butch' Wilmore – Pilot
Leland D. Melvin – Mission Specialist
Randolph J. Bresnik – Mission Specialist
Michael J. Foreman – Mission Specialist
Robert L. Satcher Jr – Mission Specialist
Nicole M. P. Stott – ISS Expedition 21 'down' crew

SPACECRAFT

Atlantis, OV-104

LAUNCH DATE

16 November 2009

MISSION

- International Space Station Assembly Mission ULF3.
- Spare parts delivered via ExPRESS Logistics Carriers.
- Final shuttle flight to transfer ISS crew members.

Left to right (back): Leland Melvin, Michael Foreman,
Robert Satcher, Randolph Bresnik; (front): Charles Hobaugh,
Butch Wilmore

The STS-129 insignia – another conceived by Tim Gagnon and Jorge Cartes with creative guidance from mission specialist Randy Bresnik – somewhat unusually features a square overlaying a circle. The square recalls the shape of the ExPress Logistics Carriers ferried on board the shuttle for this Utilization and Logistics Flight to the International Space Station (ISS). The artwork honours the achievements and successes of the Space Shuttle Program, which was by this time winding down to make way for NASA's future planned ventures in human space exploration, symbolized here by the Moon and Mars. The red, white and blue astronaut emblem projects upwards from a brightly illuminated Earth and points to the ISS at the top of the patch, thus looking to a bright future for space exploration made possible by the incalculable contribution of the Space Shuttle Program, represented by the silhouetted orbiter. The USA dominates the image of Earth as a tribute to all the men and women at NASA and its partners who make the US space programme a success. The 13 stars are for the children of the shuttle crew and the future for which they stand.

The 11-day mission, seven days of which were spent docked with the ISS, brought new supplies, spare parts and equipment to the station, including two spare gyroscopes, a nitrogen tank assembly, a high-pressure gas tank, an ammonia tank assembly, a latching end effector for the Remote Manipulator System robotic arm and more. Three EVAs were conducted during the mission to install the new components.

The STS-130 mission-patch artwork both celebrates the past and looks to the future of human spaceflight. The primary objectives for STS-130 were to deliver and install the Tranquility module and the Cupola observatory module to the International Space Station (ISS). The European-built Tranquility provides extra room, life-support systems and environment-control systems to the crew of the ISS. The Cupola observatory module, also built by the European Space Agency, is a small facility attached to Tranquility with six windows around the edge and one above allowing panoramic views in space for conducting robotic operations as well as providing breathtaking views of Earth. The mission patch is designed in the shape and configuration of the Cupola module and features the very first Earth image taken by the Lunar Orbiter 1, the first American automated spacecraft to orbit the moon in 1966. Endeavour can be seen soaring through the windows of the patch, stressing the vital role the Space Shuttle played in the construction of the ISS and in paving the way for future voyages of human space exploration.

Ten of the mission's 14 days were spent docked with the ISS. Three separate EVAs were performed to install the new Tranquility module and Cupola observatory module.

STS-130

CREW

George D. Zamka – Commander
Terry W. Virts Jr – Pilot
Kathryn P. 'Kay' Hire – Mission Specialist
Stephen K. Robinson – Mission Specialist
Nicholas J. M. Patrick – Mission Specialist
Robert L. Behnken – Mission Specialist

SPACECRAFT

Endeavour, OV-105

LAUNCH DATE

8 February 2010

MISSION

- International Space Station Assembly Mission 20A.
- Delivery of the Tranquility module (Node 3) and the Cupola observatory module.

Left to right: Stephen Robinson, Nicholas Patrick, Terry Virts, George Zamka, Kay Hire, Robert Behnken

181

STS-131

CREW

Alan G. Poindexter – Commander
James P. Dutton Jr – Pilot
Richard A. Mastracchio – Mission Specialist
Dorothy M. Metcalf-Lindenburger – Mission Specialist
Stephanie D. Wilson – Mission Specialist
Naoko Yamazaki – Mission Specialist (JAXA)
Clayton C. Anderson – Mission Specialist

SPACECRAFT

Discovery, OV-103

LAUNCH DATE

5 April 2010

MISSION

- International Space Station Assembly Mission 19A.
- Leonardo Multi-Purpose Logistics Module on board.

Left to right: Richard Mastracchio, Stephanie Wilson,
James Dutton, Dorothy Metcalf-Lindenburger,
Alan Poindexter, Naoko Yamazaki, Clayton Anderson

In the artwork, the presence of the Leonardo Multi-Purpose Logistics Module, highlighted in blue and secured inside Discovery's payload bay, tells us that STS-131 was a mission to deliver supplies and equipment to the International Space Station (ISS). Discovery is seen performing a rendezvous pitch manoeuvre in preparation for docking with the ISS. This allowed the ISS crew to observe and photograph the Space Shuttle's heat shield and check for any damage that might have been caused during lift-off. These images were then analysed back at mission control to ensure the orbiter was safe for re-entry once the mission was completed. Discovery's orbital inclination of 51.6 degrees is represented by the angle of the orbiter and gold astronaut emblem behind it. The gold star at the tip becomes the sunrise breaking over Earth's horizon, and the golden ring that completes the astronaut emblem is the orbital path of the ISS, which is shown next to it. The seven stars surrounding Earth are for the shuttle's seven crew members. Graphic artist Terry Johnson worked with the crew to create the final artwork.

The Leonardo Multi-Purpose Logistics Module carried eight tons of science equipment, experiments and supplies to the ISS and also allowed the crew to bring home a large amount of completed experiments, used equipment and waste before the Space Shuttle was retired. Three EVAs were performed during the mission for installation and maintenance work on the ISS.

STS-132

CREW

Kenneth T. Ham – Commander
Dominic A. 'Tony' Antonelli – Pilot
Garrett E. Reisman – Mission Specialist
Michael T. Good – Mission Specialist
Stephen G. Bowen – Mission Specialist
Piers J. Sellers – Mission Specialist

SPACECRAFT

Atlantis, OV-104

LAUNCH DATE

14 May 2010

MISSION

- International Space Station Assembly Mission ULF4.
- Delivery and installation of the Integrated Cargo Carrier and the Russian Rassvet Mini Research Module (MRM-1).

Because STS-132 was originally planned to be Atlantis's final flight – in the end there was one more – the mission patch shows the orbiter flying off into the distance towards the sunset. During this mission, the crew delivered the Russian-built Rassvet Mini Research Module (MRM-1) to the International Space Station (ISS), a cargo-storage facility that also added a vital fourth docking port for the Russian Soyuz and Progress spacecraft that would continue taking crews to the ISS and bringing supplies once the shuttle had retired from service. As the Sun goes down over the horizon on the patch, symbolizing the end of the Space Shuttle Program, a new day will be breaking over the International Space Station and its brand-new module. Appropriately, *rassvet* means 'dawn' in Russian, thus heralding the opening of a new chapter in human space exploration and scientific research. NASA artist Sean Collins created this captivating design with guidance from astronaut Garrett Reisman and the crew, as well as initial design contributions from Owen Evans, Shari Ciapka and the mission-patch design team of Tim Gagnon and Jorge Cartes.

Of the 12 days' duration of the mission, seven were spent docked with the ISS performing assembly and maintenance work at the station. As well as the new Rassvet MRM-1, the crew also installed the Integrated Cargo Carrier, which is used to store tools and equipment during EVAs.

Left to right: Piers Sellers, Garrett Reisman, Tony Antonelli, Kenneth Ham, Michael Good, Stephen Bowen

STS-133

CREW

Steven W. Lindsey – Commander
Eric A. Boe – Pilot
Nicole M. P. Stott – Mission Specialist
B. Alvin Drew – Mission Specialist
Michael R. Barratt – Mission Specialist
Stephen G. Bowen – Mission Specialist

SPACECRAFT

Discovery, OV-103

LAUNCH DATE

24 February 2011

MISSION

• International Space Station Assembly Mission ULF5.
• Delivery of the Leonardo Permanent Multi-Purpose
  Module, ExPRESS Logistics Carrier 4 and Robonaut
  R2 humanoid robot.

Left to right: Alvin Drew, Nicole Stott, Eric Boe,
Steven Lindsey, Michael Barratt, Stephen Bowen

STS-133 had originally been scheduled to be the final spaceflight of the Space Shuttle Program. The crew commissioned artist Robert McCall – who had designed the STS-1 insignia for Columbia's maiden voyage in 1981 – to work on the patch as a fitting tribute to 30-years of service. McCall submitted his designs to the crew, but sadly passed away immediately after at the age of 90. Astronauts Eric Boe and Alvin Drew reached out to a number of mission-patch artists, including Terry Johnson and the team of Tim Gagnon and Jorge Cartes, to submit ideas and help finalize the artwork, while staying true to McCall's original design. Alvin Drew settled on a detailed design by Tim Gagnon and Jorge Cartes after the duo spent weeks working alongside the crew on various drafts. Finally, the design was submitted to NASA artist Terry Johnson to create the final artwork for production.

The original patch featured the name of astronaut Tim Kopra, who was injured in a bicycle accident in January 2011. Stephen Bowen was assigned to replace to Kopra and the artwork was modified. The insignia depicts Discovery, the workhorse of the Space Shuttle Program, ascending valiantly into space among a cluster of stars, the six brightest representing the crew. The gold four-pointed star at the top honours Robert McCall as the main artist, while two smaller four-pointed stars to the left represent the contributions of Tim and Jorge as well as a hidden T and J in the plume. Terry Johnson added an extra J next to the T to symbolise his initials and contribution. Although two more spaceflights were subsequently approved for launch, STS-133 was the final mission of Space Shuttle Discovery.

CREW

Mark E. Kelly – Commander
Gregory H. Johnson – Pilot
E. Michael Fincke – Mission Specialist
Roberto Vittori – Mission Specialist (ESA)
Andrew J. Feustel – Mission Specialist
Gregory Chamitoff – Mission Specialist

SPACECRAFT

Endeavour, OV-105

LAUNCH DATE

16 May 2011

MISSION

- International Space Station Assembly Mission ULF6.
- Delivery of the Alpha Magnetic Spectrometer and ExPRESS Logistics Carrier 3.

The final flight of Endeavour, STS-134, was also the last planned flight of the Space Shuttle Program. (STS-135 had originally been prepared as a rescue mission for STS-134 should any damage prevent the crew from getting home.) This unique mission patch – initially conceived by Gloria Giffords, the mother-in-law of mission commander Mark Kelly – draws its inspiration from an atom. Electrons can be seen orbiting the nucleus at the centre of the patch, which also represents the birth of the universe. During the mission to the International Space Station (ISS), the crew delivered the Alpha Magnetic Spectrometer (AMS-02), a revolutionary particle-physics detector designed to analyse cosmic rays in space and seek out evidence of the phenomena of antimatter, dark matter and dark energy in a quest to discover more about the mysteries and origins of the universe. These new scientific capabilities of the ISS suggest that a new era of scientific discovery is on the horizon for space exploration and in our understanding of the universe, and this is stated in the artwork by the shuttle and the ISS in orbit over a colourful Earth limb.

Endeavour's final spaceflight lasted 16 days, of which 12 were spent at the ISS. The crew also delivered the ExPRESS Logistics Carrier 3, which was used to store several large orbital replacement units (spare hardware systems for the ISS). Four EVAs were carried out during the stay, conducting installations and maintenance work on the station. These were the final spacewalks of the Space Shuttle Program.

Left to right: Gregory Johnson, Michael Fincke, Gregory Chamitoff, Mark Kelly, Andrew Feustel, Roberto Vittori

STS-135

CREW

Christopher J. Ferguson – Commander
Douglas G. Hurley – Pilot
Sandra H. Magnus – Mission Specialist
Rex J. Walheim – Mission Specialist

SPACECRAFT

Atlantis, OV-104

LAUNCH DATE

8 July 2011

MISSION

- International Space Station Assembly Mission ULF7. Final mission of the Space Shuttle Program.
- Delivery of supplies, equipment and spare parts using the Raffaello Multi-Purpose Logistics Module.

Left to right: Rex Walheim, Douglas Hurley, Christopher Ferguson, Sandra Magnus

The final spaceflight of NASA's glorious Space Transportation System is celebrated by this simple yet elegant mission patch, designed by Margie Walheim, the wife of mission specialist Rex Walheim, to commemorate 30 years of Space Shuttle missions. Much like the mission patch of STS-1, the artwork illustrates the Space Shuttle – this time Atlantis – ascending into space shortly after lift-off with the external tank and solid rocket boosters still attached, the iconic form of the shuttle. The starry blue backdrop and red wing vector are based on the NASA 'meatball' logo as a tribute to all the people who made the Space Shuttle Program possible and confirming its status as NASA's flagship for three decades. The gold omega surrounding the orbiter tells us that STS-135 is unequivocally the last spaceflight and the end of NASA's Space Transportation System. Atlantis touched down at Kennedy Space Center at 5.57am on 21 July 2011.

STS-135 was originally the 'Launch-On-Need' rescue mission for STS-134 rather than a mission in its own right. This contingency mission, known then as STS-335, would be ready to launch into space to retrieve the crew of STS-134 should their shuttle incur damage that prevented a safe re-entry into the atmosphere. However, the STS-135 crew finally received approval from NASA to take Atlantis on one final triumphant voyage to the stars.

ARTIST CREDITS

Below is a list of all known artists, designers, artworkers and contributors who were involved with the creation of NASA crewed mission patches up to the end of the Space Shuttle Program (2011). Apologies to all the unknown artists who worked to bring us these fantastic pieces of history.

Project Mercury Artists/Designers
Cecelia 'Cece' Bibby: Mercury-Atlas 6, Mercury-Atlas 7, Mercury-Atlas 8

Project Gemini Artists/Designers
Gordon Cooper: Gemini 5

William Bradley: Gemini 7

Barbara Young: Gemini 10

Anthony Tharenos: Gemini 12

Project Apollo Artists/Designers
Allen Stevens: Apollo 1, Apollo 7, Apollo 9, Apollo 10

William Bradley (original concept by Jim Lovell): Apollo 8

James 'Jim' Cooper (original concept by Michael Collins): Apollo 11 – www.apollo11artist.com

Victor Craft: Apollo 12

Lumen Winter/Norman Tiller (final artwork): Apollo 13

Jean Bealieu: Apollo 14

Emilio Pucci/Jerry Elmore: Apollo 15

Barbara Matelski: Apollo 16

Robert McCall: Apollo 17

Skylab Artists/Designers
Kelly Freas: Skylab 2 (shown as Skylab 1 on artwork)

Barbara Matelski: Skylab 4 (shown as Skylab 3 on artwork)

Apollo-Soyuz Test Project Artists/Designers
Jean Pinataro (designer)

Jerry Elmore (final artwork for production use)

Robert McCall (the central image was based on a McCall painting)

Space Shuttle Program Artists/Designers
Robert McCall: STS-1, STS-3, STS-41B, STS-71, STS-133 (original designs)

Sean Collins: STS-30, STS-28, STS-40, STS-48, STS-44, STS-49, STS-54, STS-65, STS-68, STS-72, STS-81, STS-88, STS-109, STS-114, STS-123 (design additions and final artwork), STS-132 *Note: Sean Collins contributed to these other patches, creating final artwork files for production use: STS-26, STS-33, STS-43, STS-51, STS-76, STS-79, STS-92, STS-112*

David Russell: STS-29, STS-36, STS-41, STS-73 with Kent Rominger, STS-78 (final NASA artwork with Robert Thirsk), STS-87 with Kalpana Chawla, STS-101, STS-104 with Janet Kavandi, STS-105 with Pat Forrester, STS-113, STS-117 with Pat Forrester, STS-128 with Pat Forrester

Terry Johnson: STS-93, STS-98 with Marc Jacobs, STS-107 with Laurel Clark, STS-115 (final artwork from a design by Graham Huber, Gigi Lui & Peter Hui), STS-125 with Michael Okuda and John Grunsfeld, STS-131, STS-133 (produced final NASA artwork and submitted early design drafts)

Mark Pestana: STS-62, STS-59, STS-69, STS-83, STS-94, STS-86, STS-89, STS-93, STS-123

Brandon Clifford: STS-76

Stephen R. Hustvedt: STS-51A, STS-26

Nate Beale: STS-96

Skip Bradley: STS-51F

Rick Searfoss: STS-58 initial concept with crew (artist unknown)

Perry Jackson & Ron Garan: STS-124

Bill Helin: STS-78

Graham Huber, Gigi Lui & Peter Hui: STS-115

Marc Jacobs: STS-9, STS-111, STS-120

Richard Dann: STS-107 (original sketch design)

Carol Ann Lind: STS-51B

Michael Okuda: STS-125

Tim Gagnon & Jorge Cartes: STS-126, STS-127, STS-129, STS-132 (initial design contributions), STS-133 (additional designs to complete Robert McCall's original design)

Patrick Rawlings: STS-41G

Mike Sanni: STS-75

Gloria Giffords: STS-134

Margie Walheim: STS-135

Owen Evans: STS-132 (initial design contibutions)

Shari Ciapka: STS-132 (initial design contributions)

Although the author and publisher have made every effort to ensure the information in this book is correct, we assume no responsibility for any errors, inaccuracies or inconsistencies within these pages.

GLOSSARY

ARABSAT – Arab Satellite Communications Organization

ASI – Italian Space Agency

CNES – National Centre for Space Studies (France)

CSA – Canadian Space Agency

DFVLR/DLR – German Aerospace Center (DFVLR pre 1989)

ESA – European Space Agency

ISA – Israel Space Agency

MSE – Manned Spaceflight Engineer (US Air Force)

NASDA/JAXA – Japan Aerospace Exploration Agency (NASDA pre 2003)

NSAU – National Space Agency of Ukraine

RKA – Russian Federal Space Agency

MISSION ART **INDEX**

| MERCURY-
REDSTONE 3 | MERCURY-
REDSTONE 4 | MERCURY-
ATLAS 6 | MERCURY-
ATLAS 7 | MERCURY-
ATLAS 8 | MERCURY-
ATLAS 9 | GEMINI 3 | GEMINI 4 | GEMINI 5 |

| GEMINI 7 | GEMINI 6A | GEMINI 8 | GEMINI 9A | GEMINI 10 | GEMINI 11 | GEMINI 12 | APOLLO 1 | APOLLO 7 |

| APOLLO 8 | APOLLO 9 | APOLLO 10 | APOLLO 11 | APOLLO 12 | APOLLO 13 | APOLLO 14 | APOLLO 15 | APOLLO 16 |

| APOLLO 17 | SKYLAB 2 | SKYLAB 3 | SKYLAB 4 | APOLLO-
SOYUZ | STS-1 | STS-2 | STS-3 | STS-4 |

| STS-5 | STS-6 | STS-7 | STS-8 | STS-9 | STS-41-B | STS-41-C | STS-41-D | STS-41-G |

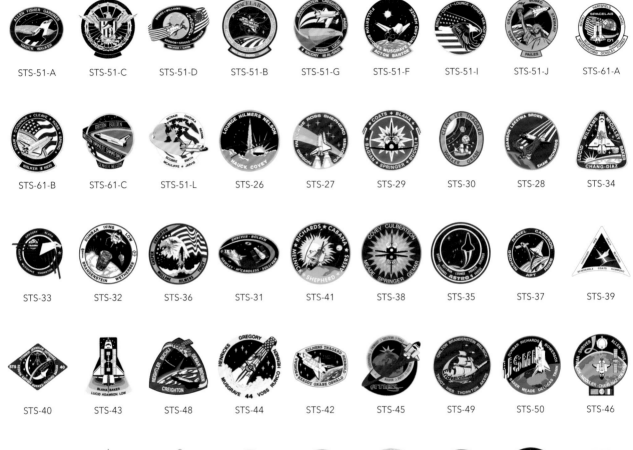

STS-51-A STS-51-C STS-51-D STS-51-B STS-51-G STS-51-F STS-51-I STS-51-J STS-61-A

STS-61-B STS-61-C STS-51-L STS-26 STS-27 STS-29 STS-30 STS-28 STS-34

STS-33 STS-32 STS-36 STS-31 STS-41 STS-38 STS-35 STS-37 STS-39

STS-40 STS-43 STS-48 STS-44 STS-42 STS-45 STS-49 STS-50 STS-46

STS-47 STS-52 STS-53 STS-54 STS-56 STS-55 STS-57 STS-51 STS-58

 STS-61

 STS-60

 STS-62

 STS-59

 STS-65

 STS-64

 STS-68

 STS-66

 STS-63

 STS-67

 STS-71

 STS-70

 STS-69

 STS-73

 STS-74

 STS-72

 STS-75

 STS-76

 STS-77

 STS-78

 STS-79

 STS-80

 STS-81

 STS-82

 STS-83

 STS-84

 STS-94

 STS-85

 STS-86

 STS-87

 STS-89

 STS-90

 STS-91

 STS-95

 STS-88

 STS-96

 STS-93

 STS-103

 STS-99

 STS-101

 STS-106

 STS-92

 STS-97

 STS-98

 STS-102

STS-100

 STS-104

 STS-105

 STS-108

 STS-109

 STS-110

 STS-111

 STS-112

 STS-113

 STS-107

 STS-114

 STS-121

 STS-115

 STS-116

 STS-117

 STS-118

 STS-120

 STS-122

 STS-123

 STS-124

 STS-126

 STS-119

 STS-125

 STS-127

 STS-128

 STS-129

 STS-130

 STS-131

 STS-132

 STS-133

 STS-134

 STS-135

ACKNOWLEDGMENTS

NASA holds a wealth of images and information available via the NASA Image and Video Library and I encourage all space enthusiasts to explore NASA's vast archives. Most of the original NASA patch descriptions which I used as my main factual source for writing about the insignias (specifically Space Shuttle) can be found at the websites below.

All photographs courtesy of National Aeronautics and Space Administration (NASA), with the exception of the Molly Brown medallion, used on page 20, which is © Heritage Auctions.

SOURCES UTILIZED FOR MISSION INFORMATION, MISSION FACTS AND PATCH DESCRIPTION FACTS:

The NASA Image and Video Library – http://images.nasa.gov

NASA Human Space Flight Archives – www.spaceflight.nasa.gov/home/index.html

NASA Main Website – www.nasa.gov

OTHER NASA SOURCES FOR MISSION DATA:

NASA Space Science Data Coordinated Archive – http://nssdc.gsfc.nasa.gov/nmc/

NASA History Program Office – www.history.nasa.gov

NASA – www.nasa.gov/missions

Kennedy Space Center's Science, Technology and Engineering Homepage – http://science.ksc.nasa.gov/history/

Original source for Mercury-Atlas 6/Friendship 7 (page 14) name explanation from *John Glenn: A Memoir* by John Glenn & Nick Taylor (Bantam)

Original source for Mercury-Atlas 8/Sigma 7 (page 16) – www.wallyschirra.com

Original source for Mercury-Atlas 9/Faith 7 (page 17) name explanation from *Leap of Faith* by Bruce Henderson/Gordon Cooper (Easton Press)

Thanks to Bert Ulrich and Connie Moore at NASA for constantly answering my questions and supplying images.

Special thanks go to the following:

Christopher Ferguson, the late Bruce McCandless II, the late Rick Searfoss, Julie Searfoss, Alvin Drew, Eric Boe, Alan Bean, Richard Dann, Leanne Price, Sam Price, Jason Hook, Jamie Pumfrey, Robin Shields and Jonathan Phillips.

Martin Pain, thanks for all your help and advice.

Gene Dorr is a space program enthusiast and has a fantastic website dedicated to early NASA patches. Gene kindly assisted me on some topics, specifically information regarding the Apollo-Soyuz Test Project patch, additional information on Apollo 9, Gemini 5, 10, 11 and 12. Anthony Tharenos supplied the Gemini 5 image, via Gene. Gemini 12 alternate design theory on crescent moon originally from *All We Did Was Fly To The Moon* by Dick Lattimer, (Whispering Eagle PR) - information supplied by Gene Dor. Gene also supplied the names of some artists. You can find his website at www.patches.genedorr.com.

Sean Collins is a graphic artist who has designed many mission patches. Sean kindly supplied me with interesting facts and information throughout production of this book, including information on various artists.

Artist Mark Pestana is a retired Colonel of the USAF and NASA research pilot. Mark worked on 9 mission patches for NASA.

David Russell is a graphic artist who contributed to the design of many Space Shuttle patches.

Terry Johnson is a graphic artist who worked on many mission patch designs throughout the Space Shuttle Program.

JL Pickering supplied some of the Mercury images. His fantastic NASA image collections can be found at www.retrospaceimages.com

Artist Tim Gagnon kindly supplied me with information on the patches he and Jorge Cartes worked on together.

CollectSPACE.com is a tremendous community for space enthusiasts and collectors created by American space historian Robert Pearlman. The website was accessed to verify the work of artists Allen Stevens (Apollo 1, 7, 9, 10), Cece Bibby (Mercury-Atlas 6, 7, 8) and Gloria Giffords (STS-134); *The Man Behind The Moon Mission Patches* by Ed Hengeveld – www.collectspace.com/news/news-052008a.html; Article on Cece Bibby – www.collectspace.com/news/news-111512a.html; and Robert Pearlman on STS-134 – www.collectspace.com/ubb/Forum18/HTML/000739.html

For Annelise. My brightest star by far... I love you.

How was the book?
Please post your feedback:
#SpaceMissionArt

AMMONITE
PRESS

ammonitepress.com

For more information on the author's work, please visit:
www.spaceshuttlebook.com